THE
ART
OF LIVING

NAWAF ALFARES

authorHOUSE®

AuthorHouse™
1663 Liberty Drive
Bloomington, IN 47403
www.authorhouse.com
Phone: 1 (800) 839-8640

Published by AuthorHouse   03/23/2018

ISBN: 978-1-5462-3001-4 (sc)
ISBN: 978-1-5462-3000-7 (e)

Print information available on the last page.

This book is printed on acid-free paper.

Contents

Introduction

"He was bitter and cruel, an alcoholic and drug addict who almost killed himself several times. Today he serves a life sentence in prison for the murder of a liquor store cashier who "got in his way." He has two sons, born a mere eleven months apart, one of whom grew up to be "just like Dad": a drug addict who lived by stealing and threatening others until he, too, was put in jail for attempted murder. His brother, however, is a different story: a man who's raising three kids, enjoys his marriage, and appears to be truly happy. As regional manager for a major national concern, he finds his work both challenging and rewarding. He's physically fit, and has no alcohol or drug addictions! How could these two young men have turned out so differently, having grown up in virtually the same environment? Both were asked privately, unbeknownst to the other, "Why has your life turned out this way?" Surprisingly, they both provided the exact same answer: "What else could I have become, having grown up with a father like that?"*

This story serves as a perfect example of that you, and only you, are the one who shapes your life. It is not your friends, nor your family, nor your circumstances that determines what type of life you live. You are responsible of living the life you truly want, and this is what makes this life exciting. No one controls you but yourself. The main purpose of this book is that I want you to realize that you are able to live the exact life that you truly

---

* Cited by Awaken the Giant by Tony Robbins

desire. It is possible. Many people have done it before you, and many will after you. Is it even worth living a life that you do not enjoy living? What is the purpose behind being where you do not want to be? No one on earth has the right to make you live a life that you don't like. Life is not meant to be lived this way. You were not born to pay your bills, stress about your financials, and remain in a constant worrying cycle. You deserve living the life that you desire; only if you do the 'work'. And here in this book, I have provided you with all of the tools that you would need in order to get the work done. You have it all within your hands. If you carefully read what is in this book, and apply the concepts and the laws provided to you, I promise you that your life will not be the same anymore. It is time for change; it is time for life to do things your way.

Please note that the language and writing style of this book had been simplified as much as possible to meet the demands of all readers and ensure that all readers benefit from the information and ideas presented in this book.

This is for you, Mom & Dad,

To Rashed Alhourani, who made this possible.
Hope the Accord cold nights were worth it.

Chapter 1

The universal laws of life

If you want to attain something, there is always a way for it. However, regardless of whether you are knowledgeable of the way of how to get it or not, you may still attain it either ways. "So why is it important to be knowledgeable of the way, if I can still get what I want without knowing the way exactly?", you may ask. Take in this scenario: You have 2 persons, Person A & Person B. Both of them want to succeed in university with a specific GPA in mind. Now, in order to achieve that goal, person A knows that there is a law that is called "the law of cause and effect", which states that for every effect, there is a cause. He knows that if he worked hard, he will reach his goal eventually. As a result, person A works hard being almost 100% certain that he can and will do it (the effect) if he worked hard (the cause). On the other hand, person B, the one who is not knowledgeable of the way on how to get what he wants, just works hard anyways and hopes for the best. Person B may or may not succeed in university, as he does not have a consistent pathway drawn in his mind that if I do this, I will get that; he lacks certainty.

The same principle and mechanism applies to the universal laws of life. There are several universal laws of life in which they provide humans "the method" to do something, and illustrate how things work on this earth. It is essential for anyone that seeks self-growth and wants to develop their self to be aware of the universal laws of life as well as to be able to critically understand and apply them throughout their daily life. The way how I see the universal laws is that they are like the instructions manual that comes with a lego toy or a new furniture, and the life you live is the lego toy; "You have the pieces and you have the tools, you just need the booklet (the universal laws) to know how things work".

Back to thousands of years ago, there were people who isolated themselves at the mountains and would study for years. Afterwards, they would teach their findings and pass these principles to people over the years. These were called mystery schools. Mystery schools were referred to the schools of these people who live in the mountains, according to Brain Tracy. A series of mental laws have been discovered by these mystery schools that are being taught just in the modern days. They have been there for a long time, people just did not use them. Of these mental laws, Brain Tracy discusses and illustrates some of the most important laws:

1) <u>The Law of Cause and Effect.</u>

This law states that for every effect in your life, there is a cause. Nothing happens by chance or outside the Universal laws. For every action, there is a reaction. This leads us to the fact that the people who are rich, successful, or famous are not the way they are because it was 'destined' for them to be so. Having all these nice houses, cars, and things do not happen from random, nor by luck (unless you were lucky enough to win the lottery). All of these "effects" are there because someone had "caused" them to happen. What makes this law very important is that it has been discovered that if you can be clear about an effect that you desire, you can trace it back finding someone else who found this effect. In other words, "if you do the same things that others did over and over again, you essentially get the same result". You can apply the law of cause and effect practically through the perseverance of the fact that **"thoughts are causes, conditions are effects"**. Use this law to increase your faith and belief in that you are able to reach your goals and dreams, and ensure that your hard work will never be wasted. If you do the cause, you will 100% get the effect, that simple.

Anthony Robbins had also mentioned this principle in his book "Awaken the Giant Within". Robbins talks about the idea of that the best strategy to reach your goals and desires is to find a role-model. Having a role model that you could literally study what they did, what do they know, how did they reach their goals, and then copy their actions and what they did along the way will not only lead you to the same results of theirs, but it will also shorten the way for you to achieve the same results; as you already have more than enough of the knowledge that is needed to acquire what you want, you just need to apply.

Our thoughts determine everything that happens to us in life – Brain Tracy

2)   Law of Belief.

The law of belief states that "whatever you believe with feeling, becomes your reality". Now, if you think about it, we act based on our beliefs, whether they are negative or positive. What is important to keep in mind is that you must be very careful of the beliefs you hold within yourself. Some of you may hold a belief that they are unsuccessful or they are not good enough in doing something just because they have failed once or twice in doing it. As a result, they never give it another shot and they live the rest of their lives believing that it is not possible. Those who are faithful enough and absolutely believe that they can accomplish something are the one who usually do it. You need to have a vision; you have to be able to feel it and see it in front of your eyes of who you want to be or what you want to accomplish. The first step to start from is to focus on what you desire, believe that you are capable of succeeding, and get rid of any negative beliefs that is holding you back from reaching your goals.

Those who are crazy enough to believe that they can change the world, are the ones who usually do. – Steve Jobs

3)   The Law of Expectation.

This law states that "whatever you expect with confidence, becomes your self-fulfilling prophecy". Your quality of life is dependent on what you personally expect to have or be. The way how you act towards your future and the way how you talk about it will ultimately turn out to be as expected. So if you expect to have a great life or expect that you will have a great product that people would want to buy, then you sub-consciously will act in that way accordingly. The main point that Tracy emphasizes regarding the law of expectation is that it is very important to always "expect the best" so things will turn out to you that way. It is also crucial to always expect the best from the people who look up to you; such as telling your child that they are going to be very successful, as this will make them raise to your expectation on a sub-conscious level.

4)   The Law of Correspondence.

The law of correspondence simply says, "as within, so without". What this means is that "the entire world around you is a mirror that reflects back for you your dominant thoughts". This law is most common in several aspects including:

➤   Relationships: your relationships with other people, especially the intimate ones, are greatly affected by what you hold into your mind. If negative thoughts are circulating in your mind, this will instantly affect the quality of the relationship and reflect back your negative thoughts on it.
➤   Income: "your outer world of income will be determined by your inner world of attitude towards money, earning, and productivity. Whatever you have in your mind about money

is directly related to your financial status. If you believe that money is the source of happiness, you will work harder for longer hours and increase performance towards earning more. If you believe that money is not a very important thing to have in life, you will not direct your senses and all of your energy and power to attain money; you will remain on a constant physical and psychological state that allows you to stay on the same level financially.

➢ Health: "your inner world of attitude towards health, food, and fitness determines your outer world of health". If you believe within yourself that physical appearance of the body is important then you will do whatever possible to maintain a good physical shape. You will work-out more often, avoid certain foods and diets, and increase your physical activity. However, if you also believe that the health state of someone could be easily damaged, you will avoid certain behaviours that negatively impact your health such as smoking and excessive alcohol consumption. The opposite is true for both cases.

➢ Success: "if you believe that you are going to be a big success on the inside, then you will see it being reflected back in your world". You will behave in a certain way that attracts success to you.

Chapter 2

Productivity Hacks

What you "think" you know isn't really true- The Dunning-Kruger Effect

As the saying goes, "the best way to trick a fool is to let the fool think that he is tricking you". Our judgement ability improves by experience, when we are exposed to the same thing over and over again. And so is the case for the Dunning-Kruger Effect. This effect says that low ability people who do not know much about something falsely believe that they are good in doing it and that they know enough (cognitive bias). This concept is very important for certain types of people such as:

> ➤ A student that does not adequately prepare for his upcoming exam because he thinks that he is good enough and that he is ready for the exam. And this is the explanation of the common phenomenon that a lot of students face during their school period (including me). The student goes over their course material over and over for a few times and then feels confident that they now know the exam material really well and that they are ready to take the exam. On the day of the exam, they feel like they know the answer to most of the questions and tell others that they think they did well. While in fact, they did the opposite. Once the student receives back their grade, they get surprised with the low mark that they have scored. It all comes back to the student not being aware

of how much material there is to be knowledgeable of and how to relate the information he had studied earlier with other pieces of information. A side note for all postsecondary school students that I would like to share with you is to keep studying until you do not feel very confident anymore about writing the exam. This is the point where you achieve the highest grades as it forces you to keep studying and expanding your knowledge as much as possible.

➢ Someone who is new to the business industry that wants to start a business. You may have the "million dollars" idea and have enough money to start up with your business but surprisingly, things start turning over your way and do not go as expected. The reason for that is that you say within yourself" how hard could it be, I already know enough", and not prepare and equip yourself with the sufficient knowledge required to start a business. Always keep asking other people who have done it before, observe around you, and make sure you are aware of the fundamental principles in the business field. Keep growing, learning, and expand your knowledge and awareness before you start.

The more you know, the more you don't know- Aristotle

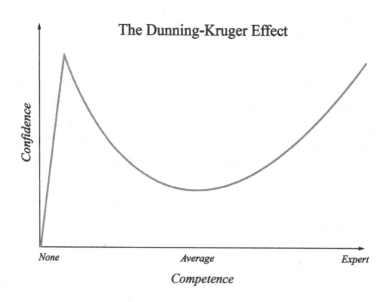

The Dunning-Kruger Effect

To illustrate further, the graph above describes the stage patterns of the Dunning-Kruger Effect. People who are not very competent and knowledgeable of something tend to have high confidence about their ability to do something. As their competency starts to increase and they become more knowledgeable about something, their confidence starts to decrease in an inverse relationship until it starts to increase again (expert level).

Unless you are extremely talented by nature in some field, keep in mind that you "always" overestimate your capability of doing something important or "think" that you know enough; and this is what will fall you into the trap and increase the likelihood of you not succeeding in accomplishing something. It is better to be over-prepared than under-prepared. When you get to a point that you feel like there is a lot of things that you are still not aware of, and there are more things to be learned, then you are probably on the right track; keep going.

The Rule of 80/20

It is a common belief that the majority of the aspects of life are proportional. The more you work on something, the better you get at it. However, this concept is not always true. Spending more time and effort on something does not necessarily lead to better outcomes. Yes, working hard is essential, but it is not enough; you also need to work "smart". A student may spend long hours of studying all of the material covered for his exam. He spends a lot of time on every specific detail in order to familiarize himself with the it. On the other hand, another student may spend even half of the time the other student had spent to prepare for his exam. He may skip some details, skim over some material, and focus on the important concepts. After the exam, both students may score the same grade, or even the latter student may attain a higher score on the exam than the former student. Even though the first student had spent much more time and effort preparing for his exam than the later one. Why does this happen?

The first student spent so much time and effort to a point that he is knowledgeable of all of the material but on a surface level. The student has so much information, theories and concepts in his head that it takes him longer to retrieve a piece of information from all of the material he memorized before the exam. Also, a simple trick in the exam's question format or structure may fall him in the trap. The other student, however, focuses only on the most important material that is most likely going to appear on the exam. The student studies the concepts that his professor had emphasized very well. He is also able to fully retrieve and use the information he had previously studied for his exam. Moreover, he does not spend much time on unnecessary examples or specific details that are not of major importance.

Up until this point, I have just explained to you the Rule of 80/20 or the "Pareto Principle". The Rule of 80/20 states that 80% of outcomes is attributed to 20% of all causes for a given event (Investopedia, n.d). Another explanation of the 80/20 as Brain Tracy has defined is that "20% of your activities will account for 80% of your results". In relation to our example above, the second student had focused on the important things (20% of the course material) that composed 80% of the exam. This theory was first introduced by the Italian economist Vilfredo Pareto, who observed that 80% of Italy's land was controlled by 20% of its population. Another example of the 80/20 rule includes:

❖ 20% of the employees are responsible for 80% of the company's success.
❖ 20% of the features causes 80% of the usage or purchase behaviour.
❖ 20% of the customers generate 80% of the revenue.

"Great Nawaf, so how can this rule be of benefit for me?", you may ask. Look into your daily life. There are certain actions and activities (20%) that you do that leads to 80% of your happiness and success. For example, the one hour a day that you spend at the gym working out or training is responsible for your shape, your physical appearance and fitness. These one or two hours a day on your phone or social media is what keeps you connected with the loves ones and up-to-date on the news and what is happening around you. These one or two hours you spend on reading a book daily is what opens up your mind and fills you with knowledge and growth; and the list goes on. It is these little things of what you do every day that leads to the great things that you live with or accomplish. Spend your time and focus on these little things (20%) that make a difference and add up to your success and happiness, rather than wasting time on the other 80% that does not make a huge impact. My advice to you is to designate 30 minutes or one hour daily; or even a couple of hours every week just devoted towards your success and self-growth. Think of new ideas or things to do that may improve your quality of life. Read different genres of books from what you usually read to expand your view of things; and reflect upon what have you done so far and plan your goals ahead of you. In contrast, stop procrastinating on the important things (20%) that you do, and do not waste most of your energy and effort on the other 80% that do not produce any results. Work less with improved outcomes!

How to do more with less time- Parkinson's law.

Parkinson's law is a term coined by Cyril Northcote Parkinson which says that "work expands so as to fill the time available for its completion". This very interesting law is essential for people who want to complete a task or accomplish something. Along with the 80/20 rule and the Dunning-Kruger effect, Parkinson's law is another productivity hack that will help you get things done, succeed more, and stay ahead of other people around you. So what exactly does it mean when you say that work expands so as to full the time available for its completion? Take in this scenario: you are the CEO of a well-known company. You assign one of your employees to a task to be done within a given time period. For the employee that you have asked him to finish the task, 90% of the work will be done just a little bit before the ending of the due date. The employee will dedicate a certain amount of time that he believes that is needed to finish the task, depending on how big it is. Even if he started working on it early, his productivity rate will be lowest when there is a plenty of time ahead of him, and will reach a maximum when there is not much time for when the task is due. So if you give him a week to do something, he will most probably start working on it after 3-4 days, get into getting things done on the 5th day, and be most productive and efficient just a day before he has to submit. What if the employee was assigned the same task but was given 2 days to finish it (which is what actually took the employee to finish it) instead of a week?

> The same amount of work has been done in both cases but in shorter time periods.

> The employee has less things going on his mind with a clearer mind which increases work efficiency (does not have to think about starting it along with other things for the whole week).

> Less effort is usually needed for the 2nd case (getting into the working place, pulling up all of the resources needed for the task, having tools necessary to work on the same task daily, etc). It is

easier for you to write a report in five hours straight in a day rather than working an hour a day for 5 days.

➤ The employee could get more things done by organizing his week into chunks. Each chunk has something that has to be done within the time period.

Important note: in the example above, Parkinson's law should be used by the employee himself rather than the employer (the employee should dedicate 2 days to finish the task when he is given a week to do so, not the employee), as this may lead to stressful working environment that could have a negative impact on the ending result.

How can I use Parkinson's law for my benefit?

Bottom line is that whenever you want to accomplish something, regardless of how big it is, restrict yourself with a specific time period and write it down in that it MUST be done within this time period no matter what happens. The time period should not be too short that it puts you in a stressful working environment nor too long that makes you waste time and energy along with working with decreased productivity and efficiency. Just dedicate whatever you believe is needed to accomplish the task without procrastination. Because if you do not restrict yourself to a certain due date to finish something, you will ultimately get it done just a little before it is due while it will occupy your mind for the whole time along with the other thoughts spinning in your head. Get it out of your mind completely and when it is time to work on it start working on it, really. Trust me, you have no idea how big an impact does this law has on your productivity level, working efficiency, and more importantly, the final outcomes.

Serial Position effect

Have you ever read a message or an email that when you were finished, you recall certain points in the message in your head that first comes into your mind when you're replying to the message? Or have you ever recall remembering certain points/ideas made while reading article more than others once you are finished reading? Well, this is the serial position effect in action. The serial position effect states that a person is more likely to remember the **first** and the **last** items presented in a series or in order, with the middle items being least likely to be remembered. This effect can be explained in that you tend to remember the things that come first due to the highest concentration of attention and the greater amount of processing devoted to them. Also, you tend to better recall the last things in a series because it is the most recent information you have processed and nothing came after it so that it is more likely that you remember it. Ultimately, the first and the last items have an advantage of being more likely to be recalled than the middle items, and this is true in every case.

The serial position effect is one of the most used concepts in everyday life. It is beneficial for a wide variety of occupations including students, employees, employers, writers, salesmen, and even business owners. It is a way of putting the essence and the focus and emphasizing the message that you are trying to communicate to the other person in a proper way. Also, it is usually the first portion of your message that imprints a first impression about what you are communicating and determines the quality of your message. For example, a student that is aware of the serial position effect knows that he must devote the best of his work on the assignment towards the first and the last parts. However, that does not mean that he ignores the middle part and not make an effort for it; It is just that place the finest of your work in the beginnings and endings because those are the ones that ultimately affect your quality of work and have the biggest impact. For an employee who has to prepare an important report to his boss or a salesman that is trying to persuade a consumer to buy their company's product: spend the most effort on the first and last parts of whatever that you are trying to write because these parts will be the highlight of your work and will increase the likelihood of achieving the purpose of the message. The first part of an article or an email is also very important because it is the piece that the other person uses to make a judgement on what you are trying to say. Remember, first and last!

The Hidden five minutes

Developing and improving yourself as a successful character starts from the little things. You may wish to be a successful person, great. One important factor is that you have to act like it. Being successful does not necessarily relate to achieving great things, or working 70 hours a week. It could also comprise the small things that we are able to acquire for ourselves. A critical point to start from is time discipline. Respecting other people's times and always making it on time is an essential feature to develop, if not already developed, for the successful character. It tells others a lot about you as a person. It shows that you have high self-discipline, and that you appreciate other people's time schedule. Furthermore, being punctual on time shows that you are a person who is reliable and trustworthy. Not to mention that being late on a meeting with someone will make things more difficult if you are trying to convince them of a product for example, or you are asking them to do a task for you.

Here is the trick: **always reduce five minutes from your appointment time.** Have you ever had an appointment that you had went out on time, but still arrived a few minutes late? Why does this happen? Well, it is simple. The answer is because of the "hidden five minutes". The hidden five minutes refers to "all of the time-consuming things that happen during the process of going somewhere". In other words, it is these couple of minutes that we are not aware of that we consume when we want to go somewhere or meet with someone. For example, suppose you had booked an appointment with a dentist on a Friday at 3:30pm. It takes exactly 20 minutes by car with no traffic to reach your destination from your house to the dental center. You leave your house at 3:10pm, but you arrive at 3:35pm. Where did the extra 5 minutes came from? Let's rewind and see what happened exactly. You left your house at 3:10pm, it takes you 30-50 seconds to walk from your apartment to your car (whether its stairs or elevator). You start your car engine and warm it for 1-2 minutes. You spend 1-2 minutes looking for parking once you arrive. It takes you another 30-50 seconds to walk from your parked car till you enter the building and find the right office/destination. You spend another 1-2 minutes at the reception signing in your papers. Putting all these "hidden" minutes together, you are late to your appointment, even though you left your house on time. And this is where the reduction of the five minutes from your appointment date comes into play. It may be acceptable to be 5 minutes late to your dentist appointment, but these 5 minutes could be a bigger issue at some cases; you are a salesperson and you have a meeting with a CEO of the targeted company for example.

You may say that I am exaggerating, and it is okay to be late a few minutes for appointments. But trust me, these few minutes that you made the other party waiting for you negatively impacts the way how the other person perceives you, on a sub-conscious level. These few minutes they spend while waiting you will be spent thinking about things like: why isn't the other person here already? Why is it me that I have showed up first and the other person didn't? etc. Which all in turn reflects back on their behavior and the way they will treat you. Again, pay attention to the smallest details, you have no clue how much of a difference they could make.

The Halo Effect

Believe it or not, physical appearance plays a large role in so many aspects of life. Regardless of whether it is a right or a wrong way of thinking; it is true. Like it or not, this is how life works. The Halo Effect is one aspect of the influence of appearance. It is a cognitive bias in which some particular positive characteristics of a person has a positive influence of the overall evaluation and judgement of that person. Meaning that if you think for some reason that a person is generous, this will impact your judgment of the person and you will automatically think that the same person is empathetic for example, or the person is honest too.

Now the largest aspect where the Halo Effect comes into play relates to physical attractiveness. Here is a great definition of The Halo Effect and attractiveness:

> "Also known as the *physical attractiveness stereotype* and the *"what is beautiful is good" principle*, the halo effect, at the most specific level, refers to the habitual tendency of people to rate attractive individuals more favorably for their personality traits or characteristics than those who are less attractive. Halo effect is also used in a more general sense to describe the global impact of likeable personality, or some specific desirable trait, in creating biased judgments of the target person on any dimension. Thus, feelings generally overcome cognitions when we appraise others." (Standing, L., 2004).

So, what does all that mean? What do we learn from this? You can take advantage of the Halo Effect in two areas:

1. How you evaluate/ assess a person overall
2. The way other people evaluate you overall

Assessing a person overall

Be careful when you judge someone's attitudes, characteristics, abilities, and knowledge. Just because someone is physically attractive or 'looks' smart that does not mean that they actually are. You may overestimate someone's ability in giving you an advice. So whenever you demand their assistance regarding something and they advise you to do something, you will instantly work with it, without even truly considering its credibility or validity. You just think that just because this person is good-looking, they must be smart, wise, and reliable. In that regard, the Halo Effect provides an advantage for attractive people; be careful from those.

How other people evaluate you

The good news is that you can use the Halo effect for your benefit. Obviously, people are not able to change how they look entirely or change their level of attractiveness, but they can certainly improve their physical appearance and attractiveness, to some level. Next time when you have a really important life event that means a lot to you, such as going to a job interview, make sure you look the best of what you can, whether by dressing your best suit, styling your hair appropriately, or keeping a fresh little white smile on your face. Do not say that your qualifications are all what matter and your appearance will not matter as much; it does. Just by making the hiring employers 'think' and perceive you as physically attractive, they will also instantly perceive you as reliable, qualified, and competent. I am not saying that you will be guaranteed of getting the job, but looking 'more attractive' will improve your chances of being hired, as you sound more suitable for the job.

The concept of the Halo Effect has also been used in marketing. This is done when well-known brands use celebrities to promote their product. When people see their admired celebrities using a brand, they instantly positively associate the brand with the celebrity, creating a more positive feeling and a sense of acceptance towards the product.

There is also another interesting area where the Halo Effect comes into play. Several studies have actually showed that if two individuals commit the exact same crime, and that one of the individuals was physically attractive while the other individual was not, the person who is physically attractive is more likely to get a lighter sentence compared to the other individual who is not attractive.

Decision Fatigue

We all have to make decisions throughout our day. Some decisions become habits, while others consume more time to be made. These decisions are made based on the best of our knowledge. We compile the various sources of information and alternatives that we have, along with the possible outcomes of a certain action, then we decide which option serves in our best interest. However, it has been discovered that throughout our day, we do not hold equal decision-making capacity.

The phenomenon is called "decision fatigue". Decision fatigue refers to the fact that our decision-making ability deteriorates gradually throughout the day after a series of subsequent decision-making. Meaning that the quality of our decisions that we make decreases as we make more decisions. We have a fixed amount of 'good' decision-making every day. This does not mean that we are not able to make right decisions once we consume the certain amount of the fixed-daily good decision-making ability; we are just more likely to not make the best decision.

This explains why Mark Zuckerberg, founder of Facebook, wears the same gray shirt every day. He actually stated that he does this so that he makes as little decisions as possible to save energy in order to serve the community. Steve Jobs, co-founder of Apple and CEO, used to wear the same outfit every day to limit his decisions and free his mind. Another well-known person who takes advantage of avoiding decision fatigue is Barak Obama, former president of the United States. He almost wears the same suit most of the time and classifies his low-priority emails as 'Agree', 'Disagree', or 'Discuss' to make space for other important decisions.

Decision fatigue can be taken advantage of in several occasions. One example could be for a manager of any type of a company or an organization who has to make the 'right decision' frequently throughout the day. Prioritizing your decision-making process so that you consume the least amount of energy and save your efforts through thinking of a more significant issues is key to improve your productivity that leads to better outcomes.

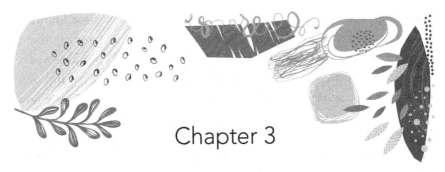

Chapter 3

Awareness is the start point for everything

Every well-built skyscraper requires a solid and proper structural base that will enable it to stand out among all other buildings. We all know the importance of the good foundational basis and the benefits that comes along with starting with the right tools. In this section, however, we will be talking about a different type of structure. It is a structure that is found in humans themselves; their spirits, their consciousness, their surroundings. It is the first element when it comes to achieving extraordinary things. It is what fuels passionate and successful people to develop and improve on a daily basis. If you ask the majority of the population what are most important factors for success, most of them will probably call out things that we hear every day; hard work, dedication, motivation, passion, etc. But there is a factor that comes before all of the previously mentioned factors, and only a few of them will name it because the majority of the population are not aware of it. And what I am referring to is **self-awareness.** The concept of self-awareness is among the most fundamental concepts in self-development. It refers to your awareness of yourself, your surroundings, your skills, and your goals. Before reaching any of your desires, or becoming a millionaire, you have to be aware of what you want first. You have to be aware of where you are at the moment, what is your current status, what are you doing in the majority of your day, how closer did you get to your goals than you were yesterday. You enter a state where you thoroughly and intrinsically realize within your inner-self what exactly it is that you want to achieve. Once you are aware and determine your desires, you have to develop the awareness of knowing how to get there, or what might increase your chances of getting there. Whether it is through educating yourself and increasing your knowledge base about that particular aspect or through practicing it over and over again until you achieve mastery in it (learning-by-doing). The way how you do it does not matter; all what matters is that you know exactly that you will reach it sooner or later. Up until this point, you should be aware that the difference between a man who earns an annual salary of $45,000 and a man who earns an annual salary of $850,000 is that the first man has developed the capacity and is aware of how to earn $45,000, while the latter man has improved his skills and developed adequate awareness and resources of how to make 850,000 a year. Every individual is paid according to the value of their service they provide, and people who earn six-figure salaries annually have the know-how knowledge base and mental abilities that qualified them to do so. And this is all done by learning and trying better ways to do something. Moreover, awareness is beneficial to various aspects in life that grants an advantage to the individual once they acquire it. For example, in the social and relationships context, a person who has developed awareness of how to deal with people or understood the different personality characteristics of the people around them has a higher chance of building and maintaining deeper social relations. You are aware that this particular person likes self-approval, so you make them hear more self-approval phrases and emphasize it when you communicate with them. Or you are aware that this person cares about physical appearance and style, so you compliment their physical appearance or when they dress well to make them feel better. In that particular example, you have to be aware of what interests' people around you; what do they care about the most. For example, complementing a self-approval-lover of their physical appearance will not be as beneficial as complementing a stylish person who likes fashion of their physical appearance, and so on. Once you are aware of what you want and what will increase your chances of getting where you want; as well as aware of your social context around you, this will grant you an advantage over people who do not know where are they in life or what they want. You could have the most technologically-advanced ship but without someone directing it, it will not go anywhere. Developing awareness of yourself and your surroundings is very important.

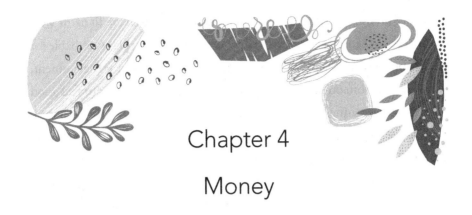

Chapter 4

Money

Why the rich are getting richer and the poor are getting poorer [*]

Have you ever wondered why the wealthy people are getting wealthier and the poor people are remaining as they are? Why is the wealthiest top 1% of the people in the world own more wealth than the bottom 90%? There must be something that is happening that creates these huge wealth gaps between people. Now, financial education is a huge topic and there is a lot to discuss and learn from it. However, I will examine and reveal to you one of the most critical financial principles that it Is a MUST for everyone to be aware of and apply as well. Along with that, I will introduce you to the incredible equation that many of us apply without being aware of its consequences.

Throughout centuries, humans purchase things based on their reasoning ability that they should own it, regardless of what the item is. Or sometimes we just think that it is nice to possess this or that; it Is nice to buy new and nice things. Even though the possession of an item in particular may

---

[*] some ideas were taken from rich dad poor dad book

tighten us on money. And that is why financing plans and credit cards were introduced. We just use our credit cards or the financing plans available for the sole purpose of buying something that we cannot afford at the moment, so we borrow from ourselves; our future earnings. It just makes us feel good to be able to get things right away and pay for them later. This is our nature as humans; we like to have many nice things. But hang on a minute, what if we want to buy all of these nice things but we do not have enough money to afford them? Then most likely we will get into a never-ending cycle of obtaining a loan to buy the item then pay back later. By the time you pay back, you will come across some more nice things, so you obtain a loan or use your credit card and buy it, and the cycle keeps going. Here is how we can prevent getting ourselves into this never-ending cycle of debit and achieve more financial freedom. What is very important to understand is that all of the things in the world are divided into two categories: the **needs** and the **wants.** There is a huge difference between the needs and the wants, and it is crucial to be able to differentiate between them in order to enjoy a joyful financial life.

- ➢ The needs are things that you NEED in order to survive. They are the things that you must have according to our necessity to live. They include things like food, shelter, clothes (unless you have lots of clothes then additional clothes are not considered a need), and healthcare.
- ➢ On the other hand, the wants are things that you want. Things that would be nice to have. They are not required, but they are more like a luxury. They include jewelry, extra clothes, electronic devices for entertainment, two or more cars used by the same person, multiple properties owned by you to spend your vacation, etc.

The difference between rich people and poor people is that rich people set their priority to acquire the needs, while poor people think that the wants are needs too. Poor people combine the needs and the wants together into one single factor: possession. They waste their money on things that they temporarily desire, but do not return a benefit for them later on. They are in a constant spending cycle; and the credit card is their best friend.

Now when the rich people prioritize acquiring the needs only, they will have a financial surplus if they really possessed the needs, and only the needs. What rich people do next is that they begin investing in the surplus of what they earned, after they have paid off the needs that are required for them to possess as a way to generate an additional source of income. Investment opportunities include things like mutual funds, real estate, investing their money in banks, buying a car and renting it, and the list goes on. Next, from the revenue generated from investing their surplus of money, they start buying a small portion of the needs, just as a way to entertain themselves and reward themselves after saving up and investing. However, they still utilize the majority of the revenue generated from investing and re-invest it into something bigger; something that generates more money for them. They start buying properties and renting them for example. Once they start making more profit from the bigger investments, they gradually expand their lifestyle and spending. They start buying nicer cars, live in nicer houses, and spend more vacations. They ultimately end up living a life that enables them to reasonably afford both the needs and the wants, while they still have an additional source of income to keep growing. However, they still use a large chunk of their investment returns and revenue and invest them again. All of these lifestyle improvements and the increase in spending is still emerging from a small portion of the investment revenue. Here is a quick example to properly illustrate the difference between rich people and poor people purchasing behavior:

Suppose you have person A and person B. Person A is the one with the adequate financial education that is considered the richer one, while person

B is the poorer one with the credit card cycle. Both of person A and person B have an income of 100$ monthly.

1) Person A spends 5 dollars on clothes, 5 dollars on food, 10 dollars on shelter, 5 dollars on bills and extra expenses. While he invests in the remaining 75$. Next month, he earns another 100$. He does the same thing and invests the 75 remaining. He does this for one year. In one year, he is investing with 900$, that generates an extra $50 for him per month. Now he makes 100$ per month plus the 50$ coming from his investment. He invests again with the 75$ he used to invest monthly plus the 50$, totaling to 125$ only used for investment per month. Gradually, he starts entertaining himself with 15$ dollars coming from investing, while is still investing the larger amount of money he makes. By time, he gets richer, is able to afford more things, and he has an additional source of income. His lifestyle starts to improve and he starts enjoying more vacations.

2) Person B spends 10 dollars on branded clothes, 10 dollars on food and dining our regularly, 10 dollars on shelter, 10 dollars on jewelry and electronics for entertainment, 5 dollars on a monthly subscription for movies and sport channels, 10 dollars for a monthly brand-new car lease, and 20 dollars on bills and extra expenses including purchasing the latest phones in market and video games etc. His mixing of the needs and the wants had lead him to pay 75$ of his 100$ monthly income in expenses. While he is only left with 25$, if not spent on something he desires. As a result of this phenomenon, poor people live poor and mostly remain at the same financial status for the rest of their lives.

Moving to our incredible equation that you must understand and apply it carefully if you want to be richer. The equation explains another reason why the rich people stay rich and the poor stay poor. It is a proof that being rich does not necessarily mean that you have more money. To illustrate, we will use a simple example. Imagine that you and someone you know are on very different financial status. You are wealthy and considered as a higher-class individual, while your friend is poor and lives below average.

- ➢ You make 20,000$ a month, while your friend makes 5,000$ a month.
- ➢ You spend 18,500$ per month from your 20,000-monthly income, and left with 1,500$ at the end of the month. While your friend is spending 2,000$ per month from his 5,000-monthly income, and is left with 3,000$ per month.

At the end of the month, which is considered wealthier; you or your friend? Just because someone makes more money than someone else that does not mean that they are richer. It is very important to understand this concept because another reason why the rich get richer and the poor get poorer is that **the rich people do not increase their spending as their income increase, while the poor people increase their spending the moment they start generating more income, so they stay on the same financial level for a long period of time.** Even if rich people increase their spending, they do it gradually and over time with a small fracture of their wealth, while poor people are more like "now as I make more money now, I can afford a newer car", for example; and this concept applies to all of the poor people spending. The more they make the more they spend.

And this explains why most of the self-made millionaires are able to make a fortune of money after they go through an economic crisis and go bankrupt. While the poor people who win a 5 million-dollars lottery spend it within a few years and mostly get back to their original poor financial state. Wealth and money making is not physical money; it is a lifestyle and a habit. It is the basic principles of money and the financial education that matters, not the acquisition of 100$ paper bills.

Money as a problem solver

During my high-school years, my biggest fear was living in poverty. I did not want to live poor. Not because I am that type of person who is obsessed with money nor I think that money is equitable to happiness. It is just that I that I had this idea of money as a problem solver. And I am not that type of person who likes problems. Let be real. Money makes people's lives so much easier. It is better to wake up in the morning, make your coffee, switch your car and listen to your favorite music while driving to work than having to wake up in the morning, wait the public transit for five minutes to arrive, having to stand up for a while until someone gets off their seat, having to listen to someone's problems over phone talking to their mom at 7am or some homeless drug addict recklessly shouting random music lyrics on the busy bus. That is the simplest example I can provide you regarding money as a problem solver. It just makes your life easier. What is more important than viewing money as a problem solver is viewing it out of self-respect. What more could you ask than self-respect? Let me explain to you more. Referring back to the driving vs public transit example, when you work hard enough to afford driving to work daily rather than using public transit, you are respecting yourself. You are providing all types of comfort for yourself. When you want to bring happiness to your wife by buying her a nice piece of jewelry, but you are unable to do so because you cannot afford it, you are not respecting yourself. How would you allow a physical object such as a money bill to prevent you from bringing happiness to your life? Who on earth has the right to deprive you of the ability of doing things that you like to do? There is absolutely nothing that has the right to do so. And here comes again the relationship between money and self-respect. When you earn enough money that enables you to be have freedom of choice of doing and purchasing whatever you like, taking vacations and travelling as much as you like; again, you are respecting yourself. The feeling of incapability that emerges from you not being able to afford putting your children in the best educational environment, or not being able to afford a nice house for your parents as a way of payback and an appreciation for what they did (you could never fully pay back your parents of what they did), or dinning out and travelling for vacations regularly with your family should be what drives you to have self-respect. When you consume one meal a day because you cannot afford to eat three little meals a day, then you are not respecting yourself. Look everywhere around you and will find the association between self-respect and money; even to as simple as fruits and vegetables. When you do not enjoy the taste of different fruits and deserts because it may impact your budget, then you are not respecting yourself. As simple as that. You must get to a level that money does not prevent you from doing anything you like. Money should not be an issue for you. You should not worry about when your next rent is due or when the hydro bill is above usual. Life is not meant to be lived this way; it is a much nicer place. If you are at this situation currently then it is okay, but what is not okay is that if you do nothing about it. What is not okay is that if you do not act up and improve your current situation and raise your standards of living. Be the master of yourself, Attain your desires, and live life fully. Life is too short to live it on a budget.

If there is only one situation where being selfish is acceptable, then it is when it comes to money. Be selfish in asking for a nice car that comforts you. Be selfish in asking to live in a fancy 5000 sq^2 house with an outdoor pool and a backyard. Be selfish in dressing the top-quality brands and most suitable. Be selfish in that you do not want to work for someone else and that you want to be the boss of your own self. Be selfish in acquiring all of the things that you desire. You deserve attaining all of you desires, you just have to work for it. The people that have already achieved their desires are no better than you. Keep in mind that you only live once. Try to make it worthwhile. Try to enjoy as many things as you can during your lifetime.

Try to explore new places and taste new food. Travel, explore, and enjoy. All of these things are cost money. Life is too boring to be lived poor.

"We say that money is not important, then we work 8 hours a day". - Brian Tracy

Money is Only Part of the Game

People mainly refer to money when you ask them to define being rich. They would list all the different categories that relate to financial freedom such as owning a house or multiple properties, driving exotic and fancy cars, and have a six-figure number sitting in their bank account. However, this definition of being 'rich is partially true but it is only part of the equation. Wealth is used to define the individual's success because it is physical. It shows when someone is financially free, and this is all what the majority of people care about nowadays; looks and appearances. Another reason why wealth is associated with the individual's success is because it is not easy to earn money. It is not easy to build your own brand or provide a service of value that enables you to get paid a six-figure salary. Becoming a millionaire is not the typical norm. Having a million dollars is not the common thing to be adopted by people. The average person earns far less than a million dollars annually. However, this does not mean that becoming a millionaire is impossible nor it is a black or white area. If you develop the skills and learn the principles of financial freedom and apply them, you could easily make your first million.

Being a millionaire is only designated for people who are willing to do what it takes to make it. it is only meant for people who are ready to sacrifice a lot of things throughout their lives to become wealthy. It is for those who take the courage to ask for the first million. Those who believe in themselves and are able to overcome all of the obstacles and failures during their journey. Money is deserved. It is earned. It is a reward for the very high self-accomplishment and discipline. It is not meant for average people who quit right after their first unsuccessful attempt.

Keeping all those perks that come along with being rich, financial freedom is only part of the game. A large amount of people who become single focused on making money that gradually develop a limited vision of life (only caring about making more money) become so obsessed with money that earning more money becomes their ultimate goal. It is all what they care about. They just want to make more money no matter what. And this is a very dangerous stage to be at. Making money is a great thing until it reaches a point where you make money on other things expense in life. For example, money is an enemy of you when it forces you to spend extra hours to get things done when you should be spending quality time with your family. Money is an enemy of you when it forces you to work overtime in a way that negatively affects your physical and mental health, where it becomes all what you think about most of the time.

Money is important, but there are other things that are important too. I always ask myself: "how rich do I want to be"? or "to what extent do I want to be when it comes to wealth"? what is the satisfactory amount of money to me? And after several years I was finally able to find an answer. I want to earn enough money that will enable me to not worry about money anymore. It is hard to make an exact estimate of how much money one wants to earn, but a level where you could live your life without financial worry is a good target to aim for. Not so much money, but not too few. It is always good to travel and explore other things in life or practice things that you like and enjoy doing. Get some time for yourself and the beloved ones too, it is very important.

Approach money as a supplementary object that will make your life easier. That will make you live a happier life. Not something that will totally take over your life; something that will control your life and destroy your time, health, and family. Jack ma, the richest man in China, and the founder of Alibaba was asked once about what does he regret the most throughout his successful life. He answered "I regret a lot of things. I regret that I was working so hard spending so little time with my family". He continues, "my wife once said: you do not belong to me, you belong to Alibaba".

When I first watched this video of him, I was shocked. I kept on reading the sentence about what his wife had told him over and over again. It is a very powerful statement full of meaning behind it. that video was an eye-opening for me that I felt that all of his billions of dollars that he had earned were of no value, because it was made on other more important thing's expense; family. I mean, what is the use of travelling on a private jet or living in a multi-million-dollar house if you had sacrificed your family-time for it? It just feels so empty.

Actions and value are proportional: some basic economics.

During my first year at university, I decided to take an economics class that introduces students to the basic principles and theories in the field of economics. I had and still have a huge interest in predicting human behavior and actions before they make it. But what I did not realize is that this economics class I took had served me more than just a background in economics. It helped me conceptualize the idea of what drives our actions. What makes us behave in a certain way. It is a very simple concept that if you understand it properly and apply it, it will enable you to be aware of two things:

1) The ability to understand your behavior
2) The ability to develop a broader understanding of other people's behavior

The concept is that **our actions are driven by what we value the most.** In other words, we do certain things based on how much value do we assign to these things. And this explains why drug addicts are willing in some cases to commit crimes, steal, and use aggressive force so that just their supply of the drug does not seize. As the drug provides them with intense high and euphoria, they value it so much in that they put acquiring the drug as a first priority. You may see very wealthy people but they dress very ordinary clothes, wear little to no accessories/ watches, and use public transit. While on the other side, you see average singers or actors that only wear very expensive brands, their body is covered with all the different types of gold and diamond accessories/ watches, and drive luxurious cars. Does that mean that the very wealthy people are not actually wealthy and the average singer/ actor is very wealthy? The answer is no. It is just that the singers/ actors give an enormous amount of value toward their physical appearance and how they look in the eyes of others, while the very rich people give little to no value to how they look or how they show up to the public. It is important to note that there are wealthy people who buy expensive clothes and drive luxurious cars. It is not that this is the case for everyone but it could be that the wealthy people also highly value their physical appearance. Let us narrow our scope and get personal a little bit. Say there is a girl in her teenage years that would like to pierce her nose, but she is worried that it may not look good as expected, or piercing her nose may be eye-catchy that people will not make her feel comfortable in public. The only scenario that she will most likely pierce her nose is that when **she values having her nose pierced and the desire to do so more than she values other people's opinions or what other people will think of her.** And that is our problem. We give more value to less important things in life and we give less value to the more important things. It is very important to assign the real value to things and not exaggerate or lessen the actual value of things. And the only way to be able to assign the real value to things is throughout ourselves. What do we care about the most, ignoring everything else. Therefore, it is critical for us to be aware of our thoughts, our beliefs, and our personal principles and standards so that we do not make poor judgements or unsatisfactory decisions. Another point that we must be aware of is that we can take an action or prevent taking a certain action if we increase or decrease how much value we give to taking or refraining from taking an action. Doing this will enable you to have greater control over your actions and understand your behavior. If you wanted to really make a certain action then you should know that deep within yourself, you highly value doing that action and vice versa. The same thing applies to other people's actions. If you see someone who really wants to do something, then you could conclude that this "something" means a lot to them and they highly value it.

Chapter 5

The essentials in Body Language[*]

Knowing the essentials of the body language and what do they represent or mean is one of the most important aspects of self-development. Being aware of the fundamentals of the body language helps you in both effectively expressing yourself and appropriately understanding others. Several psychology and body language studies and researches have shown that communication between human beings occurs 20% through the words you say (speech), 30% through your tone when you say it, and 50% through what you do with your body when you say these words. I referred to the word 'essentials' of body language in this chapter because it will give you a brief knowledge of body language. There are various concepts and postures in body language. However, I will be only covering the most fundamental and common throughout our daily lives.

There are so many examples of when body language can be beneficial. You can apply what you learn about body language in almost every aspect of your life. Here are some examples:

- Suppose you have an important interview coming up and you really do not want to miss the opportunity; whether it is a job interview or an interview for a grad application at a university. No

[*] cited from The Definitive Book of Body Language by Allan and Barbara.

matter how good of a speaker you are, applying the proper body language and bodily positions that flow agreeably with what you say and how you say it will definitely improve your chances of being selected over other applicants.

- Suppose you have to present a presentation or give a speech publicly somewhere. Implementing the appropriate gesture and standing properly while presenting will reflect a positive image of you as a person and what you are trying to communicate, even if the content of what you were presenting was not that good.

> *Being aware of basic body language is an essential part for the ideal professional and social identity that is required for building a successful character.*

Here, you will learn some of the major indicators of some of the most common inner bodily expressions that are usually not revealed through speech. These include:

- Spotting the liar.
- Signs of interest.
- Things to do/ not to do in your first job interview.
- How to leave a good first impression when you meet someone for the first time.
- Different postures (sitting, standing) and their representations.

Again, it is important to note that what is more critical than understanding/ reading the person in front of you is knowing what not to do or what to prevent for your own body language. Read yourself before you read others. Another important point to keep in mind that it is difficult to rely on a single bodily expression to conclude something, as many body language postures overlap and may have more than one meaning. What you can certainty depend on is the exhibition of a few of body language expressions that were made collectively.

How do I know if someone is not telling the truth?

- ➤ Liars usually smile less.
- ➤ Liars blink more frequently when they tell a lie (blinking is also a sign of stress as we will discuss later on).
- ➤ Liars tend to cover their mouth when they lie. This reaction emerges from the sub-conscious mind as a response of trying to hide the truth. However, when someone covers their mouth when they are listening to someone, it indicates that the listener who is covering their mouth do not believe the person who is talking.
- ➤ Liars tend to touch their nose in a fraction of a second. The explanation of this reaction is that studies have demonstrated that when someone lies, their nose blood vessels contract and the blood pressure increases. As a result, the person touches their nose very quickly in order to elevate this little disturbing feeling resulting from the increased blood flow.
- ➤ Rubbing the eye. Individuals tend to rub their eye when they are telling a lie as a response from the sub-conscious mind that a person does not want to be in the situation they are put currently, so they try to hinder their presence. Rubbing the eye also comes as a response from the person telling the lie to prevent their self to look at the person being lied to. Liars also tend to intentionally keep a firm eye contact with the person being lied to, as a response from them that if the liar maintains strong eye contact, the person being lied to will not have any suspicious that the person is lying.
- ➤ scratching the side of the neck, behind the ear in particular. It is common for people who are lying to rub behind their ear using their index finger (this expression most commonly comes along with lying about being sure of something). For example, when someone tells you "Yes, I understand what are you talking about" and rubs behind their ear at the same time, they probably have no idea about what are you talking about.
- ➤ Changes in pitch or tone. Higher than normal or lower than normal tones during speech may reveal that the person is not telling the truth.

How do I know if someone is interested in me?

You may like someone, but you're still not sure if the feeling is mutual with the one you like. Knowing the body language of the signs of interest enables you to stay aware of the people around you that like you. However, these signs of interest vary across males and females yet there are some common signs of interest that are similar for men and women. Firstly, we will discuss the signs of interest that are exhibited by women followed by the signs exhibited by men. An important note to keep in mind regarding men and women is that **males show the features of the opposite sex when they are interested in females and vice versa.** For example, women will stand in an oblique way, bend their waist, and play with their hair in order to catch the man's attention. On the other hand, men will stand up straight, tighten up their chest, and speak with a deeper voice tone.

Sings of attraction for females towards males:

> Raise her head and pull her hair backwards on the shoulders. This is among the most common signs of female attraction in which it sub-consciously demonstrates how women take care of their look and their beauty in front of men.
> Crossing the legs in a parallel fashion. Women tend to cross their legs in an attempt to attract men's attention through looking more feminine. However, crossing the legs could also mean that the person is embracing a defensive/ negative position. As mentioned earlier, it is important to examine a collection of signs at once to confirm your body language inference, as there are many overlapping body language signs that have totally different representations.
> Playing with her hair. A common body language behaviour a woman shows when she is interested in a man is playing with her hair; usually in a curly fashion. This body language sign could be

translated in that when women play with their hair, they are subconsciously trying to draw men's attention towards them.

<u>Signs of attraction for males towards females:</u>

- ➤ Constant eye contact. If a male is interested in a female, they will make constant eye-contact with her. This is largely because males are more visual beings than females. Believe it or not, men are more physically attracted to women than women are attracted to men.
- ➤ Good-humorous teasing. Men usually use playful teasing in an attempt to express their interest when they are attracted to women. This is because men are less emotionally-expressive than women. Most of men find a difficulty in expressing their real emotions towards women, so they use teasing as a form of flirting.
- ➤ Body postures. Look for non-verbal bodily postures of the male such as where the feet are pointing, raising his eye-brows frequently in an attempt for him to show you that he is interested in what you're saying —shock-, or straightening his back and widening his shoulders as a way of expressing his assets and dominance (confidence, reliability, authority).

Things to do/ not to do in your job interview

Nowadays, the workforce has a pretty competitive environment that favors the people who are most qualified for the positon. Several factors may influence your chances of being hired; including previous job experience, educational background, and other qualifications. However, another determinant factor that greatly influences your possibility of being hired is how well you perform at your job interview. You may not have the best educational background, nor have top qualifications yet you may sub-consciously imprint a positive impression through your body language that favors you over many others for the job position. Here, I will provide you with the most important things to keep in mind during your next job interview. These include:

1) Walk with energy. Studies have shown that it takes approximately seven seconds for humans to judge a person when they first meet them. So, make sure you direct these first seven seconds for your benefit.

2) Mimic the body language of the person who's interviewing you. This is referred to as 'mirroring' in body language. Mimicking someone's gestures, speech, and attitude is like a way of saying 'we are alike'. Once people develop feelings of similarity, there is a higher chance for building understanding, mutual trust, and empathy within each other.

3) Maintain eye contact. Maintaining a strong eye contact sub-consciously improves the sense of communication between you and the other person and keeps it tight. Avoid staring at the wall or the floor during conversations; this distracts both you and the person who's listening to you.

4) Your sitting position reveals a lot about you. Make sure that your shoulders are spread out, back is at 90 degrees, and neck is straightened. This position greatly reflects confidence and capacity.

5) Always keep your hands open and visible; put them on the table for example. In the science of body language, open hands imply honesty and enhances feelings of comfort to the other person.

6) Do not cross your legs or your hands. Crossing the legs/hands is a body posture that reflects a negative state of the person doing it. This gesture is also embraced by people who are in a defensive position. Try to avoid crossing your legs/hands as much as you can.

How do I leave a good first impression when I first meet someone?

We are in a constant cycle of meeting new people throughout our lives; it is just part of our human nature. Some people may become more than just "strangers" right after the first meeting, others may never be seen again. It both cases, it is important to leave a good first impression the moment you meet someone. Building new relationships is happening either ways; might as well get the most out of it. Some of the most important steps for imprinting a good first impression when you first meet someone are:

1. When you first meet someone, call them by their first name. A person's name is the most beautiful sound they would like to hear. Not only it makes them feel good and cared for, but also it directs their attention toward what you're saying. Using a person's name when talking to them is a very effective way of grabbing someone's attention; making them become more involved in the process of communication, acknowledging their identity, and feeling more valued.

2. Get personal. Studies have shown that it is more likely for someone to get along and be more comfortable chatting with you if you let them talk about themselves personally; people will be more open. It's even better if you could find similarities between both of you on a personal level. Be careful though, do not get too personal.

3. Avoid exaggeration. Do not over-act or over-react in trying to laugh or keep the conversation going. This will leave a sense of 'faking' that will leave the other person uncomfortable and make things awkward so that they just want to roll with the conversation; which as a result, makes the conversation lose its value. It makes it feel like you are trying so hard to keep up with the conversation rather than actually having a proper one. Keep things natural and let it flow.

Negative body postures to avoid

As mentioned earlier, body language can reveal a lot about what is inside our minds and how do we think about something. In this section, we will discuss some of the most common body language behaviours that are simple but carry a lot of meaning behind them. Being aware of these postures will work in your favor by either implementing them to emphasize what you are trying to deliver, or to avoid negative body language positions that leaves a negative image. These behaviours include:

1. Avoid placing your hands in your pockets. Putting our hands in our pockets reflects a 'closed-situation' body language. This means that whenever someone has their hands in their pockets, or do not have their hands visible in general, that they are requesting their own personal space and do not want to be engaged. Hands-in-pockets gesture sends a "I'm within my own bubble" signal, and it indicates for others to not be involved with them.

2. Avoid crossing your arms. It reflects a defensive position to others and a sense of not liking the current social situation. Crossing your arms is like saying 'I don't like where I'm right now". It's also a sign of un-openness and isolation.

3. Avoid the rapid movement of your hands/ legs. It reflects a sign of nervousness and 'impatience' to others. As a result, it makes others uncomfortable as they start to think that you just want to finish the conversation and end the interaction with them. Moving your hands and legs rapidly translates to 'jump to conclusions, I've got other things to do'.

Different body positions (sitting, standing) and their meaning

Now, the fun part that makes body language more interesting is that you can read others around you without them having to say a word. The behaviours they exhibit and their body positions may reveal enough about a person. In this section, we will examine different body positions and their interpretations.

1) *The relationship between the feet and the brain.*

Body language experts have found that the direction of the legs and the brain are closely linked together. For example, if you are standing with a group of people, give a quick glance at their feet and you will be able to tell which direction their brain is thinking of at the moment. If a person has one foot directed towards someone, then in most cases, they are interested in them. Another person who has their foot faced towards an open space within a group of people, then this means that they want to leave; and so on. Furthermore, crossing the feet while standing is a representation that the person is comfortable at the moment and is planning to stay where he is and no going anywhere.

2) *The pupil of the eyes.*

Experts at body language concluded that the human eye dilates up to four times when the person is encountering excitement, and contracts when the person has anger or negative feelings. Furthermore, it has also been demonstrated that the eye pupil and sexual arousal are directly linked, meaning that when a man looks at a woman and think that she is attractive, his eye pupil dilates. Same principle is true when a woman looks at a man that she thinks is attractive.

3) *Crossed arms.*

Generally, anything that is crossed reflects a "closed" or a defensive position. It emerges as a sub-conscious response from our body to try to 'block' the words coming out at us from others using our arms. For example, when parents rebuke their child for doing something bad, the kid will mostly embrace a defensive position through crossing his arms.

4) *Quick and frequent blinking.*

Observing the person's blinking rate is one of my favourite and most used body language expression. Blinking frequently and at a quick rate for a short period of time is an expression that is associated with either stress, lying, or both.

5) *Rubbing the fingers or closed palms.*

One of the major body language indicators of stress is when someone rubs their fingers, or when someone has their palms closed. It is important to be aware of the "stress indicators" as implementing them strongly displays to other people on a sub-conscious level that you are stressed. Therefore, the best way to not reflect a negative image to other people that you are stressed during presentations or public speaking is by being aware of these body behaviours, then learning how to avoid them.

6) *Placing one of the hands on the chest.*

Body language experts have revealed that one of the major signs of honesty and comfort (other than open hands) is when someone put one hand on their chest when they say something. So next time when you are trying to convince someone of something or trying to prove that you "did not do it", putting one of your hands on your chest will greatly increase your chances of being convincing. Another sign of honesty is opening both of your arms while slowly flipping your hands; just like your trying to hug someone, but with a lower arms-level.

"Learning body language is not only about reading others, but it is also about you doing the appropriate body language expressions so that you can effectively deliver your message and communicate, or to avoid the expressions that may contradict what you're trying to say".

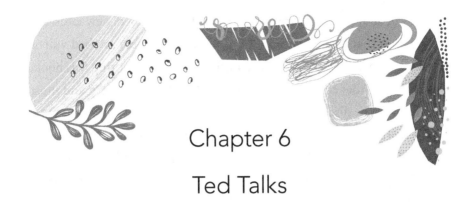

Chapter 6

Ted Talks

In case you don't know, TedTalk is a 10-20 minutes' speech or presentation that is presented by people who are experts in their field from all over the world. Ted Talks is a non-profit organization that is devoted to spreading ideas that aims to improve the world (citation). These people try to deliver the most important ideas and information of their knowledge in a relatively short period of time so that it keeps the audience's attention.

I was scrolling through Facebook one day and I came across a video talking about goal setting and the importance of staying focused. The video was a little bit long so I decided to watch it before going to bed. However, I left the video playing and fell asleep before the video has ended. On the next morning, I woke up and still had some of the main points and ideas that were in the video stuck in my head, so the first thing I did was to write down the interesting points that were mentioned in the video that I have watched. The reason for that is that if you want to hold a new belief or effectively absorb information, it is best to say or listen to it just right before going to sleep. At that time, your body is resting and so is the "conscious mind", while the "sub-conscious mind" is peaking and reaching its most active state (we will talk more about the conscious and sub-conscious mind later in the book). Since that day, I have developed a habit of listening to podcasts or audiobooks before going to bed. The amount of new ideas and information that I have acquired from listening to these pre-bed videos was totally worth it. Therefore, when I first thought of writing this book, the first thing that came to my mind was delivering the main and most important ideas, discoveries, and studies from the speeches presented by experts in TedTalk videos. In the following paragraphs, I will present to you a few of TedTalk videos that I personally think are worth sharing. I would advise you to refer to the original video for any idea or piece of information that is of interest to you.

1) **The first 20 hours: How to Learn Everything.**[*]

In this video, Josh Kaufman talks about how the experience of having a child and being a parent started taking a lot from his time and made him busy. "I am never going to have free time again", he complains. To Josh, becoming a parent and not having free time has created a huge problem, as he "enjoys" learning new things more than anything else. In an attempt for tackling this problem, he spends hundreds of hours researching and exploring "how long does it take to acquire a new skill". Ultimately, Josh came to the conclusion that it takes 10,000 hours to learn something new and be good at it. However, the 10,000 hours rule applies to expert-level performance, meaning that on average, it takes 10,000 hours to be on the top of the elite class of performers in an ultra-competitive field. Now here's the interesting part: the number of hours that are needed learn a new skill and be "reasonably good" at it is twenty hours. 20 hours of deliberate focused practice is all you need to be good at something.

In reflecting upon what Josh have found from his studies, think about all of the times you wanted to learn something but you refrained from doing it because you were "too lazy" or "did not have time for it". What more powerful and compelling motive are you waiting for? It only takes 20 hours to learn a new skill from scratch that you have never ever done before! I do not want you to only read the previous sentence, but also sit back for a second and feel it! It takes 20 hours to: learn how to play on guitar or piano, learn how to ski or play tennis, or even learn how to be an effective communicator or a public speaker. Think of all the different aspects of your life that you could learn and improve; how great would that make you feel about yourself acquiring these skills?

---

[*] full video can be accessed at https://www.youtube.com/watch?v=5MgBikgcWnY

2) **8 traits of successful people**[*]

"Informational speaker", as Richard St. John likes to call himself. During Richard's trip to California few years ago, when a teenage girl coming from a below medium-class family was sitting beside Richard on the airplane. Richard pulls up his laptop trying to finish up some work. In the meantime, the little girl looks at Richard and keeps asking questions, like she wanted to get somewhere in life. Suddenly, out of the blue, the girl asks Richard: "are you successful"? Richard answers the little girl and the questions keep going. This random conversation between Richard and the little girl on the airplane drives Richard to explore further to examine what makes people successful. After 10 years of research and over 500 face-to-face interviews with successful people, and the collection of thousands of other success stories to contextualize the topic and to ensure that all sorts of sources were collected to know what really makes people successful. Richard concludes that there are eight common traits that all successful people have in common; or "the eight to be great", as Richard calls them. More people said that these are the factors that made them succeed more than anything else:

1. Passion (love what you do)
2. Work really hard
3. focus on one thing; not everything
4. keep pushing your self
5. come up with good ideas
6. keep improving yourself in what you do
7. serve others something of value
8. persist, because there is no success overnight

"The 8 traits are really the heart of success, the foundation. Then on top, we build the specific skills that we need for our particular field or career; such as technical skills, analytical skills, etc", says Richard.

---

[*] full video can be accessed at https://www.youtube.com/watch?v=NOl0v54DaXo

You are fortunate enough to have all of Richard's findings and long hours of hard work presented to you on a plate of gold. Therefore, if you really want to succeed, which I believe that you do just by the fact that you are reading this book at this moment, it is important for you to shed the light on these 8 traits and develop the skills necessary to reach your goals.

Chapter 7

Focus on the outcomes

We all want to accomplish great things; things that have never been done before. Things that are of value for us and to the people around us that provide us with a sense of fulfillment; a sense of self-satisfaction and happiness. Whether it is career success, financial related, or personal relationship building, it does not matter. What matters is attaining what we desire and making our dreams come reality. However, throughout the process of working on our goals, we tend to fall into a major mistake without realizing it. This mistake often negatively affects our capacity to produce outcomes and excel at something. It even prevents us from reaching our ultimate desires, in some cases. **We usually pay more attention towards the process of accomplishing something rather than the outcomes of it.** This in turn negatively impacts our motivation to do something as well as it creates a sense of avoidance for us towards that particular task.

During my senior year at university, it was the final exams session and I remember heading home from university. It was sometime around 4:00am in the morning, and while I was walking towards my car at the car parking, I came across a senior year friend that I have met during my frosh year. "what are you doing this late at school?", I asked him. He replies, "man, I have had enough. This is just way too much". We continue talking about school and he keeps complaining and telling me how hard it is to keep up with school work, how much course information he has to study, how difficult it is to keep on working with other project group members, how he has little quality time for himself to spend, and how his diet and sleeping cycle is all messed up during exams. He could spend all night complaining and talking about the negative aspects of being in university and getting education. He was so focused on the negative side of school that being in school almost became a bad thing. After he's done talking, I reply: "what about getting paid a decent salary and being more prone to promotions and career developments after you graduate? I know that life may not always be in your favor, but it is because there are other more important things that are about to happen that will change your status quo. That is what is costs to hold a higher education degree, otherwise everyone would get one. You can never get something of value without effort; keeping in mind that effort and value are always proportional; remember that". I continue, "you could struggle for 4 years then live a proper life for the next 40 years, or you could enjoy your 4 years without getting anything done, and struggle for the next 40 years; your call". It is understandable that a university degree is not a necessity in order to be successful or wealthy, and that there are so many millionaires, even billionaires, that do not even hold a high-school degree. But also keep in mind that this is an exception, not the common norm. What is the percentage of people who are millionaires that do not hold a university degree? One in a 1000? One in a 10,000? Who knows. While on the other hand, what is the percentage of people who are millionaires who hold a university degree? There is an interesting quote that is written on the wall of Harvard's University's library that says:

"Time the study pain is temporary, has not learned the pain is life-long".

And this is the mistake that most of us fall into that reduces the quality of our work and in some cases, prevents us from reaching our goals. The reason for that is our psychological and mental state is very important when we try to accomplish our goals. Focusing on the negative side and on the process of attaining something rather than the positive side and the outcome of something puts us in a disadvantaged position. It de-motivates us and makes us lack a sense of perfectionism in performance in which ultimately, affects our outcomes. I mean, let's face it. you are doing the work either ways, why not do it while being in a positive psychological and mental state that will improve the quality of your work? Bragging about how difficult things are will not get you anywhere other than making your life more challenging.

Be careful of what you focus on while you work on a task, as it will clearly show in your outcome. The next time you work on something, focus on the outcome rather than the process. Alter your attention from the struggles you are facing to the rewards you will get, and you will see how easier things become to accomplish. It will fuel you with just the sufficient motivation to get done whatever you are trying to achieve.

Chapter 8

Human Behavior in terms of pain & pleasure

It is well known that we as humans are not random living spices. Each one of us has a series of logical reasoning and way of thinking to act in a certain way. Furthermore, **our behaviour is mainly determined by what we hold in our minds- our thoughts**. In the case of any event or a situation that requires us to act or react, we instantly build on what we already know about something and what is the most appropriate response- according to our mind- to adopt; then eventually, we take action.

A person is largely known for their actions. We know that Bill Gates knows how to act in a certain way that generates wealth. We know that a good person is the one who donates to charities and the needy people and gets involved into volunteer and community work. We also know that "bad" people are the ones who commit crimes and steal from other people; regardless of the background of both people. Even though the word "good" and "bad" has a broad meaning, it is just used as an example to illustrate. Over the course of life, we do things over and over that ultimately turn into habits. These habits shape our identity. On the other hand, we tend to do so much just to avoid experiencing certain events (illness for example).

While I was sitting on the coach reading some of the books the other day, I came across a very interesting concept developed by Anthony Robins in his book "Awaken the Giant Within". In his book, Anthony says that "Everything you and I do, we do either out of our need to avoid pain or our desire to gain pleasure". Meaning that all of our actions are determined by either to avoid pain, to gain pleasure, or both. You go to the gym because you feel like being in a fit physical shape gives you pleasure. The smoker smokes his cigarette because he feels that it is gives him pleasure. A person may work his ass off in school and get a college degree because he wants to avoid the pain of not being able to find a job. And this is why you see that a cocaine or other drug addicts are willing to do anything they could possibly do (even commit crimes in some cases) to get another dose of the drug; it pleasures them. The more likely something is going to provide you with pleasure or avoid pain, the more you are willingness and desire to do it.

How can I benefit from this concept?

As mentioned earlier, everything we do is either out of our need to avoid pain or our desire to gain pleasure. This concept is very useful for people who want to form new habits or quit their previous ones. All you need to do to apply it is to associate what you want with enormous pleasure while also relating not having it to enormous pain. Doing this over time is very powerful to gain more control over your life. Let's take smoking for example: if you are a current smoker and willing to quit smoking, the first thing you have to do in order to quit is to stop associating smoking with pleasure. That first cigarette puff is not pleasurable anymore; it does not make you feel better and it is not a stress relief anymore, etc. Next, you must associate continuing of smoking to cause you excessive pain. Imagine yourself laying on that white hospital bed with the oxygen mask on your face and the nutritional pipe is pumping nutrition drops from the plastic connected to your arm. Think of all the bad things that may result from you continuing to smoke. Think about your family, your children, your parents, and how would they feel if you were diagnosed with some type of cancer or a chronic illness. Generate as much pain as possible. Once you have cut out the pleasure produced from smoking, and associated enough pain resulting from smoking, you will be more likely to be able to quit the habit.

It is important to note that in order to double the chances of you successfully quitting a habit and not relapsing, It is advised that you replace it with another habit. In the case of smoking, keep your mouth busing with chewing a gum or something for the first period of time until you completely lose the habit.

Chapter 9

Your Inner Peace

All of the big accomplishments had been achieved by great people; people who are fully aware of their surroundings and how things work. These people are the ones who are experts in self-control and discipline. They are able to direct their minds toward what they desire, and block the undesired. Personally, I believe that living a proper financial, social, or even academic life really requires a healthy mind to be present in the first place. All of the great things happen in the right settings and under the right circumstances in which there is no disagreement between the person and their mind, their thoughts, and their emotions. They all flow in harmony consistently and the person is able to direct and control them to some level.

One of the most important aspects of a healthy mind is the "feel good emotions". It is the ability to embrace a pleasurable self; or at least, avoid feeling unhappy or depressed. Wayne Dyer talks about you being able to choose how you want to feel in your everyday life; in his book, "Your Erroneous Zones". The way how he views it is that you may think that certain things or certain people are the ones that are behind your unhappiness; they are the ones that make you feel bad about something. While in fact, **it is you, and only you, who is responsible for your happiness.** It is just your way of interpreting these people besides all of the thoughts that you create in your mind about certain things or people that make you feel unhappy.

Take In this example:

you have an old, dusty car that you use to go to work daily. This car runs great but it is just not the best out there. On the other hand, your neighbor purchases a brand new luxurious car that you have always wanted to have. Now, you have two possible scenarios:

a) You start having negative thoughts within yourself about your car and your financial situation and you are no longer satisfied internally with your car, although you still drive it.

b) You completely understand that physical material is not an indicator of wealth nor financial status; it just emerges from different personal preferences and different financial management within people. You are satisfied with your car as long as it fulfils its purpose (transportation).

Looking at the example above, if you undertake option A or option B, you are still driving the same car in both cases. What changed is "the way how you feel about it". Thus, you either drive while being appreciative, optimistic, and satisfied with what you have, or drive while feeling ashamed, depressed, and unsatisfied. **It is the feeling that changes, nothing else.** Luckily, this freedom of choice is available for each one of us. we are able to have full control over how we feel about something. All you have to do is just think differently. Change the way how you view things and always try to look at things from a different angle. Once you change how you think, your thoughts will change. Once your thoughts change, your emotions will change. Once your emotions change, the way how you feel about something will change and you will have a completely different experience of life.

> *"I can control my thoughts. My feelings come from my thoughts. Therefore, I can control my feelings". citation*

Bottom line is that you the one who is responsible of how you feel. If you think and view things differently, you will ultimately be able to change and control how you feel which in turn grants you greater self-freedom and self-control.

Chapter 10

Passion, Passion, Passion!

As we were born, we all had a certain interest towards something in particular that we grew up with it. Whether it is a type of sport, communicating with people, something financial-related, or even knowledge. A few of people have continued pursuing their passion with enthusiasm, while many others have allowed life to take them over. These people who kept on doing what they were passionate about; something that provided them with a sense of excitement, were ultimately the elites in their field. They spent hundreds, if not thousands, of hours working and learning. They are in a constant improvement cycle. They get better every single day.

What differentiates someone who is doing something that they are passionate about from someone who is doing something that they are not passionate about is the will to sacrifice. People who are pursuing their passion are willing to make huge sacrifices just for the sake of acquiring what they desire. The reason for that is that "**they love what they do**". They enjoy every bit of it. They are willing to spend huge amounts of time and effort continuously doing what they love to do. During the process of doing what you love, you are will prefer to be working on what you are passionate about instead of doing something else. You would rather be working on something that interests you till very late hours at night than enjoying sleeping early. The will to sacrifice your sleep hours emerges from the sense of passion towards finishing something; and so on. Furthermore, there are some phases in life that it is very difficult to proceed and keep moving forward unless you love what you do, because if you do not, you will quit at the first obstacle. Passionate people get to a level that they do not see anything within their vision except their goal. They pay little to no attention to all of the other barriers that come in the way. They are always focused. There is this glorious hidden power that emerges from their passion, which keeps pushing them to the next level. The greatest things in life that are out there were all accomplished by passionate people. Only passion is what enables people to do extraordinary things that were never done before. Remember, it is very important to be passionate about what you do in order to succeed in it. Otherwise you will most likely live average just like many others.

As Steve job once said, the reason why it is very important to be passionate about what you are doing is that if you do not have passion, it is so hard to not give up. If you do not do what you love or enjoy what you are doing, you will ultimately give up once things get more difficult. You will not have the energy to proceed forward and just quit because you do not love what you are doing and think that it is not worth it; you do not value it enough that you really want to acquire or achieve it.

"Nothing great in the world has been accomplished without passion." – Georg Hegel

"Passion is energy. Feel the power that comes from focusing on what excites you." - Oprah Winfrey

"Passion is what gets you through the hardest times that might otherwise make strong men weak, or make you give up."- Neil Tyson

Chapter 11

Do not compare yourself to others

We were born equal. There may be some differences in our IQ's or genetics favoring some individuals over others; but ultimately, what matters is hard work and dedication. There are several examples supporting that hard work is the most important factor among all the factors leading to success. For example, we all know that both Messi and Ronaldo are great soccer players. But these two characters have become elite class soccer players and reached success in different ways. It is a known fact that Messi is a talented player. He was born with it. Messi has been a skillful player since he was young. There is no doubt that he has worked really hard to become what he is today, but talent was the determining factor in his case. On the other hand, Ronaldo was not as naturally talented playing soccer. There is no doubt that he had little talent, but what made him reach the level he is at today and be compared among the best soccer players in the world was his hard work and dedication. His soccer skills were very average compared to other kids in his age when he was a child. As he grew older, he kept on training and focusing on one ultimate goal: becoming the best. Keep in mind that I am not arguing who is the best player in the world here, I am just using real life examples to illustrate how hard work plays a major role in expanding your chances of succeeding to reach your desires.

Imagine with me for a moment that the life we live in today is a blank A4 paper. On this paper, there are many different horizontal bars. Each bar corresponds to a specific category. For example, bar number one is the bar of skills needed to earn money and financial education. The second bar relates to the bar of relationships and communication. The third bar correlates to sports and physique; and the list goes on. To further understand the point, here are what may be the other bars compromised of:

➢ Bar of creativity.
➢ Bar of business.
➢ Bar of self-discipline.
➢ Bar of decision making.
➢ Bar of playing on instruments.
➢ Bar of writing ability.
➢ etc.

Each individual pursues the bar that interests them and the one that they are good at during their life. With enough time and effort spent at a certain bar, they reach the elite class in their area of expertise. Take in Warren buffet for example. Warren have always had a passion towards numbers. He loved dealing with numbers and interpreting the true meaning behind each number. He developed his skill and passion to get into stock trading and investments; that ultimately, made himself a fortune out of his passion and became one of the wealthiest and best investors throughout history. In Warren's case, he spent more time on the bar of money, stock trading, and investing more than he did on any other bar. Bottom line **is that people who have reached their desires are the way they are today because they have spent more time and effort than the rest of other people in their field.**

"It's not that I'm so smart; it's just that I stay with problems longer."- Albert Einstein

People who are great communicators are so because they communicate a lot. Professional sport players are the way they are because they have spent an enormous amount of time training.

Do not compare yourself to more successful people to feel bad and start blaming others. The only one whom you should blame is yourself. Do not let the success of others bring you down or make you lose hope; use other people's success to fuel your desires and motivate you to reach whatever it is that you want to achieve. Use the success of others to make you believe, if you do not already do, that it is possible; that you can reach your goals and your ultimate desires.

Chapter 12

The Table of Beliefs

While I was reading "Awaken the Giant Within" by Anthony Robbins, I came across a very interesting concept. As we all know, it is very important to be confident in many aspects of your life in order to accomplish extraordinary things. The long journey that you will have to go through to achieve your goals will require you many things along the way. Your character must be equipped with various tools during the process to successfully overcome every hurdle and obstacle that you face along the path. Establishing the proper set of beliefs about yourself and figuring out what you really believe in and who you really are is a good place to start the equipment.

Robbins defined the "belief" as "a feeling of certainty about something". Then he introduced that idea that if we control our beliefs, we will have more control over our lives. The question here is: **How can we control our beliefs?**

We can control and decide what beliefs we want to carry regarding ourselves. We are also able to emphasize a positive belief and deemphasize a negative one. This is done through a concept that is called "the table of beliefs". The basic idea here is that we have to transform thoughts into beliefs; once we do, we construct a new belief. How is that done?

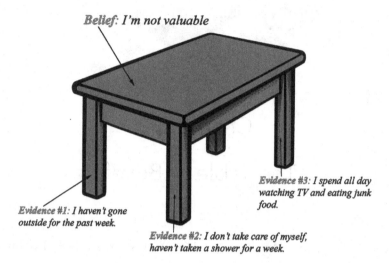

Belief: I'm not valuable

Evidence #3: I spend all day watching TV and eating junk food.

Evidence #1: I haven't gone outside for the past week.

Evidence #2: I don't take care of myself, haven't taken a shower for a week.

Imagine that a belief is the surface of a table. And all of the references, past experiences, and the basis that occurred throughout your life to hold that particular belief is the legs of the table. The surface of the table (belief) without its legs (past events) remains constant on the ground without any profound effect. The more legs we attach to the table (past experiences and references), the more stable and firmly the table will stand (beliefs we have). You can use this concept to acquire more positive beliefs and empower yourself, or obtain more negative beliefs and depower yourself. It is all under your control.

Chapter 13

Be mysterious: Always conceal your intentions.

Be open in your mind but do not be open to people. This is the key feature of what I personally call "the elastic character". Generally, individuals like other individuals who complement them, make them feel good about themselves when they are around, and rarely criticize them (be aware that constructive criticism is not included when I say "criticize" here; that is a totally different case). **Be mysterious,** let others talk about their actions and provide their opinions about things without judging them. Or at least, do not show that you are judging them. Let others talk about their different habits and lifestyles; where they live; what music they listen to, what is their opinion on something, etc. Being a mysterious person will grant you two major advantages:

1) People will keep on talking and uncovering their personal thoughts to you, because you made them guarantee that you do not judge people. This will help you to broaden your view of things and people, as well as being more understandable and acceptable of the psychological and habitual/ behavioral differences of people around you (which again falls into the features of being an "elastic character.

2) If you make people more open to you by concealing your intensions and judgements, you will be interacting with the truest

version of the individual. They do not have to think twice before saying something nor they will eliminate some things they were about to say just for the fear of being judged. This will help you understand the person more and know what interests them; what do they like and what do they dislike; which ultimately assists you to improve and tighten the relationship between you and the individual.

Chapter 14

Reinforce the positive attitude

Being able to properly deal with people is one form of intelligence. You come across different people and different personality types, and you have to deal with each one of them differently. Different mentalities, characteristics, environments and way of thinking. Now, I may not be able to put together all of the aspects of the successful character for dealing with people, but I will cover a very important concept that will make your life much easier.

Whenever you see a positive attitude, complement it. The reason for that is that by complementing the positive attitude, you are opening doors for the production of more and more of the positive attitude. Additionally, a positive frequency will emerge between you and the other person that as a result, will create a positive energy. The concept behind the positive attitude is that when you complement a person for their positive attitude, you are informing them that they are being watched. Their actions are noticed, and that you are aware of their behavior. Once you complement their positive attitude, they will sub-consciously behave more positively and more frequently in front of you because you have demonstrated to them that you are observing them. They do so to receive the same positivity and acceptance along with the feelings of well-being for being told what they were told before (complement).

It is important to magnetize the people that are with positive attitude especially those that they and you have shared interest in common. I remember in 2017 when I along with a few friends launched the first student online store in London, Canada (StudentOnlineShop.com). I and one of the co-founders, "Junior", had the same job responsibilities, more like co-workers. He did not have a professional attitude towards the business nor he had time punctuality. And this is totally understandable as we were still university students and had not got into the real market, yet. However, I used to complement him every time he does something good. Whenever he shows up on time for meetings, I say, 'always right on time Boss', stuff like that. Whenever I ask him to send me a report or some sales-related documents and it happens for him to be in a good mood and not on a busy-schedule, then he takes his time and prepares the documents very professionally with excel sheets, I compliment him, more like "this is very professional, I like it" or "did not know you were that good in preparing stuff". Surprisingly, I have noticed a major shift in his behavior and attitude. He started to always be coming on time; documents were always perfectly prepared, and so on. I started to realize that the more I complement his positive attitude, the more positive attitude he had. It just made him feel good every time I told him good things, so he started doing more good things, and this slowly became a habit for him. But be careful to not over complement or over-react, this will take you to the opposite direction.

Chapter 15

The guy at Mercedes-Benz

There was a Mercedes show store nearby where I used to live. As I am a big fan of the German cars, I used to stop by to look over the newest arrival models every while and then. But this time, it was not like every time. I walk into the store and find a neat salesman approaching me. 'How can I help you today'? he asks. As it turns out that we both were Mercedes fans, we find ourselves jumping from one conversation to another. Long story short, he opens the back door of an S-600 Mercedes Benz AMG, one of the most expensive models in the show store, and says: have a seat. I take the driver seat while he sat on the opposite side of the car from the back seat, looking through all over the car and feeling the soft, comfortable hand-crafted Paige leather, and starts talking. He takes a deep breath, sighs, and says: "where do I start from?" He started giving me advice on life and how easy it is to make money and live financially independent, it is just that people do not think and use their minds. People do not set pre-determined goals ahead of them and try to purse them, they just live their day and tall about how rich they would like to be. They want a lot of things but when it comes to actually working for it, a few take action. Then he starts talking about the importance of being and remaining focused on your goal. I spent two and half hours talking with a complete stranger, sort of, about something that both of us were passionate about; success, aside from the new Mercedes S 500. That day, he told me something that had never been out of my mind since he said it, and

It keeps coming to my mind whenever I slack off doing things or feel de-motivated. He said:

> "you know when you take a little girl with you and she comes across a toy that she really likes and she just holds it tight through her hands? That she just wants it and nothing else but the same toy? You even try to tell her that I will buy you a better one but she refuses, and sticks on her mind? And if you take it from her, she starts crying, yelling, and rolling over the ground, devoting all of her energy into obtaining the toy. That is how consistent and determined you must be towards what you desire. That is how focused you must be to achieve your goals. This spirit and sense of focus and consistency is found in every one of us; we were born with it, but we just do not want things that bad, we just kind of want it. We do not want things as bad as this little girl wants the toy, that is why most people are not successful".

Since then, this little girl has stuck in my mind until this moment. It reminds me to stay focused and never give up on my dreams. Try as hard as you can, just do not stop trying. Ignore what everyone says, ignore what everyone thinks about you, because you, and only you, are the one who is able to get you wherever you want to be.

Chapter 16

Repetition loses value

In economics, the term "scarcity" refers to the limited availability of a commodity, usually a commodity that is high in demand. For this purpose, the science of economics is mainly focused on how to properly allocate resources in the most efficient way while considering that most resources are scarce. **The more something is unavailable or limited the higher it is demanded and the more value is assigned to it.** For example, the two brothers, De Beers, own most of the diamond industry in the world. Technically, diamond has no value. It is just a compressed carbon deep into earth. What they did is that they have formed a monopoly to control the diamond industry. After that, they have limited the supply of diamonds and the quantity sold, so that they can increase its value and sell it for a higher price. Through effective marketing strategies, they were able to associate diamond with longevity and social status, as it has a precious shiny look and it could last forever if you took care of it. Ultimately, diamonds sell for a relatively high price now. Another example is a strategy that some automotive brand owners use to assign a higher value to their cars produced. Fancy car companies such as Bugatti and Royce Rolls produce limited edition cars that only 100 or 500 were produced from them worldwide; which in turn creates a sense of distinctiveness and uniqueness to the consumer and a desire to own one of them as a way to reflect social status. Again, less available= more valuable.

So how does this apply to human interaction and behavior?

What is interesting is that the concept of scarcity can be applied to humans too through self-availability. Do not always be available to others. And by that, I do not mean to ignore people around you or to hide in your room and never show up again. It just that do not always stick around with the same individuals. Get to know more people in your life so that your presence will decrease for the people around you, or just give sometime for yourself alone. Give some time to reflect upon yourself and evaluate your life, decisions, and actions. Develop awareness of yourself and others and have a more in-depth realization of where you are at the moment and where are you going towards in the future. Have some time for yourself to learn from your past, evaluate your present, and plan your future. Being less available to people will add meaning to your presence. It will enrich the conversations with people around you. The thoughts and ideas you exchange with other people will become more interesting because interesting things will be communicated more often as there will be less time for the less important/interesting things to say. And on a side note; they will miss you more.

Another important area where scarcity applies to individuals is that do not always be the one who is talking. Listen more than you speak. Being talkative Is not a bad thing, it is just that talking a lot decreases your chances of saying something important, unless you were Toney Robbins. It also increases your chances of saying something foolish, or putting yourself in an embarrassing situation due to saying something that was unnecessary. **Silence will add more value to your words once you spit them.** However, this does not apply to your loved ones, family or very close friends.

Chapter 17

Do not get attached.
Maintain your freedom

Life consists of an interaction with different individuals, different objects, different feelings, and the list goes on. Each one of us has their own habit that they enjoy doing, or someone who they love being with, or even a series that they like watching. But what matters here is not the person nor the show, it is our feelings towards it. We may say that we love someone, and that we would sacrifice anything for them; but in fact, we do not love the individuals themselves, **we love the way that being with this specific person makes us feel**. We love it when they care for us, when they ask us how did our day go, when they laugh at our jokes, etc. We love a person because they make us feel special. They make us feel valued; they make us feel good about ourselves. The same concept applies to the all other things in life. Wealthy people buy exotic cars not because they like the car itself, but because they like the feeling the car gives them when they drive it. They like the feeling of sitting in a comfortable leather seats, or listening to the V12 engine sound accelerating, or even they like the public attention it provides them once they drive their fancy cars in the streets. In some cases, wealthy people trade physical money for certain feelings when they buy a fancy car or gold-plated phone. It provides them with a sense of uniqueness and differentiates them from other people. In that sense, you have to acknowledge that it is you, and only you, who is responsible for your happiness. If you want to give away something that you are used to, all you have to do is to stop associating positive emotions towards it, and watch the magic happens. You do not have to drive a brand-new car to be happy, nor you have to live in a fancy house to be happy; all you need is change the way of how you feel about something. However, that does not ignore the importance of money. Yes, money does not equal happiness, but it equals a lot of other fundamental things.

Chapter 18

You Can't Jump the Stairs

Knowing what you want to achieve and having determined goals is essential, but what is also essential is how you view them and how you have them sorted in your mind. Be careful of how you approach your goals in your mind. Setting big goals is good, but it may discourage you to work towards them if they are 'too big'. On the other side, setting small goals may not get you far enough; they may be too small that they barely produce a significant change in you. The best way to set your goals is as follows: set a huge goal that you really desire and care about the most, but view it as a long-term vision in that you acknowledge that it is not possible to make it happen today, tomorrow, within a month or even a few months. It takes time. This goal should be where you see yourself within the next 5-10 years for example. What type of person would you like to be in the future. Examples of this type of goal include starting up your own company, being a minister or a politician in the government, being a well-known scientist, or even building a strong social connections network. **This is called the long-term vision.** However, in addition to the long-term vision, you must set short term goals that will help you to get to your long-term vision. These goals must not be too small nor too big. These are the small pieces that when compressed together, are your long-term goal. Setting up short-term goals is critical because it will fuel your success throughout your journey. It will motivate you because you will feel accomplished once you achieve one of them. It will also motivate you to achieve more of them because you will psychologically realize that these mini-goals are achievable. Examples of the short-term goals may include finding a proper job that will improve your financial status, working-out daily at the gym, finishing a 10-hour training session of some type of skill or a musical instrument, etc. **this is called the short-term vision.** Now here is the interesting part: keep your longer-term goals in mind but focus mainly on the short-term goals. Collectively, your focus will shift from the long-term goals to the short-term ones, but these short-term goals are the little pieces that make up your long-term goal. So that you will reach your long-term goals through the short-term goals spirit/vibe. You will get to a point in your life that you realize, "hey, reaching my long-term vision is closer than I thought". But in fact, it is not closer; you were just working towards it with a focus on the short-term goals.

I remember when I finished high-school, my mini-goal was to improve my very basic English language abilities so I can get into a well-known university in Canada. Once I got in, my goal was to pass first year. I did not really care about my GPA. During my last two years at university, my goal was graduate with a competitive average so I can complete my education and get my MBA at a prestigious university. Who knows what is next? All of these mini-goals collectively made up my long-term vision, and will ultimately get me to what I have in mind. Maybe if I focused on attaining a competitive average and getting an MBA during my first year, I probably would get discouraged and give up; who knows.

Chapter 19

The Law of Attraction

This chapter is probably one of the most important chapters written in this book and has the greatest potential to influence your life. The law of attraction is a broad topic that is multi-dimensional and has a lot of branches. There are even entire books talking solely about the law of attraction. However, the concept of the law of attraction is very simple. I will be covering all what you need to know about the law of attraction as a start; the basics and fundamentals, how it works, and how you can use it for your benefit. You can always read more and find additional resources about the law of attraction if you would like to go further in-depth about this topic. I highly recommend reading 'The Secret' book or watching 'The Secret' film by Rhonda Byrne. This book is one of the best-selling books covering the law of attraction.

Very few people are aware of the Law of Attraction yet some of them use it knowingly or unknowingly. This law can impact your life in several aspects, including health, wealth, relationships, and success. The main idea behind the law of attraction is that **your thoughts become your reality.** Whatever you hold in your mind continuously and repetitively will ultimately come into physical existence in your life. The Law of Attraction basic mechanism derives from the fact that the universe is composed of particles of energy that vibrate, and that everything on earth has and is made up of energy. Which also means that human's thoughts have energy too. Whenever you think of something, you are creating energy signals and vibrational forces that are of the same frequency of the energy that the physical objects contain, that is sufficient to bring your thoughts into existence. Obviously, just for the fact that you think of something for a few seconds or think of a random thought you had for once does not mean that it will come into your reality. There are certain rules and things that must be done in order for your thought to have an impact towards your world. Thoughts have to be repetitive on a constant basis, accompanied with the absolute belief of that thought. The more frequent you think of something and more repeatedly throughout your day, the more likely it will translate into your reality. Emotions also play a key role in fueling the Law of Attraction: the more emotions you associate towards something, whether positive or negative, the more likely it will come into existence. Furthermore, the Law of Attraction is neutral in that it does not distinguish between positive or negative thoughts. Positive thoughts bring positive circumstances, and negative thoughts bring negative circumstances.

So how can I use the law of attraction?

It is pretty simple. There are several ways in which you can practically use the Law of Attraction. These include:

- ➢ Visualization/ imagination
- ➢ Self-affirmation
- ➢ Repetition, frequency, and emotions
- ➢ Fake it till you make it
- ➢ Write down your thoughts

1. Visualization/ imagination

This is among the most powerful techniques of using the Law of Attraction. First, you have to put yourself in a relaxed state, both physically and mentally. This can be done through laying down on your bed with comfortable clothes in a room with appropriate temperature; not too cold not too hot. It is recommended that you take off any jewelry that may disturb your attention or comfort, including any hand watches or bracelets. Close your eyes and take deep breaths for about 1-2 minutes regularly until you feel that you are in a very relaxed state. Once you do, you have to visualize yourself as you already have what you desire, with many details as possible. In an example of wanting a certain car for example, visualize yourself pressing on the unlock key, hearing the unlock car peep, and seeing the orange unlock flashers of the car flashing once or twice. You hold the chrome door-handle, and enter the car. You can smell the fresh smell of a brand-new car. You feel the luxurious steering wheel through your palms. You also feel the comfortable brown-leather seat of your own car. You look at the window and see people staring at you and your car. You are just feeling good. This is just a quick example of how your visualization process have to be. Remember, you have to feel as you already have what you desire, with as many details as possible. The more frequent you visualize the better. Your mind does not distinguish between your thoughts and your reality. Also, if done properly, you can actually feel the same way that you would feel in real life if you properly visualize what you desire through your imagination. By visualizing, you are enabling your mind to create an energy that is equitable with the energy to bring it into your physical world. It is important to note that you can visualize anywhere anytime, but this is the most effective and appropriate method to visualize effectively.

Quote: imagination is more important than knowledge.
Imagination is everything. It is the preview of life's coming attractions.

2. Self-affirmation

A lot of people may think that a person is crazy or has some mental-issues when they see them talking with their selves. However, the opposite is true. Talking with yourself is an effective way to approve and confirm a thought that you hold. It actually makes you believe what you say over time and is a great source of energy that has a direct impact on the person. You can try it. Stand in front of the mirror, look at yourself and slowly speak up some positive statements such as: 'I'm confident', 'I love myself', 'I'm beautiful', 'I'm wealthy', 'I'm in a perfect health state', etc., and you can feel the positive impact these positive statements have on your psychological state, mood, and how you feel after saying these affirmations to yourself. These statements have a certain energy that you are producing that matches the energy vibrations of these statements being actually true.

3. Repetition, frequency, and emotions

As mentioned earlier, the more frequent you think of something and the more you repeat the process, the greater your chances are of translating these thoughts into reality. Repetition is the fine line between keeping your thought as just a 'thought' or brining your thought into the physical world. More frequent = more energy. However, whenever you think of something repeatedly, make sure that you accompany it with emotions that will make you absolutely believe your thought and ultimately, attract it into the physical.

4. Fake it till you make it

We all have heard of this saying before, but never actually knew where it came from. This is a very simple technique yet effective to attract what you desire. If you want something, you have to act like you have it already throughout your day. For example, if you want to be wealthy, you have to talk like you have millions of dollars already, dress like you are one already, feel like you are rich already, and so on. This will trick your mind as you are wealthy already, and it will attract wealth energy vibrations into your life, as your mind does not differentiate between what is real and what is not.

5. Write down your thoughts

By writing your thoughts on a paper, you are translating the thoughts in your head into the physical world; something that can be seen. This will clear your mind of what you really desire, and will keep you focused by knowing what exactly do you want. Reading what you wrote every day for a few minutes is also very effective because you are combing self-affirmation with written thoughts.

Chapter 20

The sub-conscious mind

The subconscious mind as the driving force behind everything in your life. Think of the subconscious mind as a huge empty fertile soil. Whatever you harvest in it will get you the same result as what you have harvested. Your beliefs about yourself is what you harvest, whether positive or negative, and you will eventually see the result in your life of what you absolutely believe in. You can also get rid of the negative beliefs about yourself. It is just a fertile soil that accepts whatever you put in it, and will ultimately, make you up as a person.

To better understand the subconscious mind, you have to know how your mind works. We all know that the brain is the most complicated organ in the human body. Thousands of research and studies are done on the brain every year, and yet we still do not understand it fully. However, fortunately, the basic properties of the brain are well-known and comprehended, and I am going to share it with you briefly in this chapter.

The human brain is composed of two main parts: the conscious and the subconscious mind. Each of these have their own roles and functions differently. However, the subconscious mind is the driving force behind everything. It is what enables humans to achieve extraordinary things that may seem impossible until someone accomplishes it. Generally, the conscious mind is responsible for the following:

➢ Reasoning, logic, and thinking.
➢ Thoughts.
➢ Physical movement.
➢ Will power.
➢ You daily life interactions/responsibilities.
➢ Decision making.

While on the other hand, the subconscious mind is responsible for the following:

➢ Huge memory storage of your life.
➢ The internal organic processes in your body (blood circulation, breathing etc.)
➢ Feeling and emotion.
➢ Beliefs.

Keep in mind that both the conscious and the subconscious mind work interactively, but the subconscious mind is way more powerful than the conscious mind and is responsible for the great things that people achieve, if programmed properly. Dr. Murphey said in describing the difference between the conscious and the subconscious mind:

> "the conscious mind is like the navigator or captain at the bridge of a ship. He directs the ship and signals orders to men in the engine room, who in turn control all the boilers, instruments, gauges etc. The men in the engine room do not know where they are going; they follow orders. They would go on the rocks if the man in the bridge issued faulty or wrong instruments. The men in the engine room obey him because he is in charge and issues orders, which are automatically obeyed. Members of the crew do not talk back to the captain, they simply carry out orders.

> The captain is the master of his ship and his decrees are carried out. Likewise, your conscious mind is the captain and the master of your ship, which represents your body.

Environment and all your affairs. Your subconscious mind takes the orders you give it based upon what your conscious mind believes and accepts as true" (The power of your subconscious mind book, Joseph Murphy)

How does the sub-conscious mind work?

The sub-conscious mind is a machine that receives orders, and applies them. It does not have the ability to judge whether these orders are good or evil, nor it differentiates between what is in the best interest of the person. This is why it could be a double-edged sword in cases. Another critical feature of the sub-conscious mind is that it does not have the ability to differentiate between imagination and reality. Meaning that if you imagine something properly, you will feel like you have actually experienced what you had imagined. Which is a basic functional property of the sub-conscious mind. One of the well-known and most effective methods to use the sub-conscious mind is through imagination. When you imagine something correctly and very precisely, with as many details as possible, your mind will not be able to know that you are imagining it. once done frequent enough, your mind will start to translate what you imagine into reality and devote the life's circumstances and events through the universal laws of life so that you ultimately reach your desires. Another effective way of employing the sub-conscious mind for your benefit is through repetition with emotion. Note that emotions are the fuel of the sub-conscious mind. If you think of something repetitively throughout your day, and associate it with emotion, you will ultimately acquire it. this is why you have to pay close attention to your thoughts throughout the day; they collectively shape your reality. A great way to remember the mechanism of the sub-conscious mind is through using this formula that I use on a daily basis:

Thoughts + emotions = beliefs.
Beliefs + repetition= reality.

When to use the sub-conscious mind?

As you now have an idea of what the sub-conscious mind is, it is time to know when to use it. The general principle is that your conscious and sub-conscious minds operate in total opposite situations. Your conscious mind is at peak when you are in your full energy state. When you are most alert and conscious. In contrast, your sub-conscious mind is at peak when you are lowest on energy, both physically and mentally. When you are in a comfortable state that requires zero energy consumption. There are two situations where your sub-conscious mind is at peak and most active; which therefore, produces best and quickest results. These situations are:

1.   the 5-10 minutes before you go to sleep.
2.   the 5-10 minutes after you wake up.

For the first situation, as you go to sleep, your body starts shifting gradually from the conscious to the sub-conscious state. As you go to bed, you slowly begin to lose attention around you, your blood pressure decreases, and you become more rested and comfortable. At this stage, you are not using all of your five senses. Therefore, your consciousness decreases. As your consciousness decreases, your sub-consciousness starts to rise. This is where your sub-conscious mind is most active and ready to receive instructions from you. The same process applies for the second situation. During the first 5-10 minutes after you wake up, you are somewhat still in a sleepy-like state where your awareness and attention are at a low level. This is where your sub-conscious mind will be at their peak state and starts decreasing gradually as you prepare to start your day and get out of your bed to start using your five senses and requiring your consciousness to be present.

Chapter 21

Avoid Complaining

We all encounter several life events throughout our lives that we may not like. Whether it is being rejected from a job interview, going through an embarrassing situation, getting into unnecessary arguments fueled with anger, or even being fined with a speeding ticket. All of the previously mentioned scenarios and many other events are normal; they are part of life. Life has its ups and downs. You can never expect to be happy and feeling well all of the time. However, what is important is not these life events. Rather, it is the way how we approach these negative circumstances and react to it. Whenever you encounter a negative life event or a stressful situation, you have two options in reacting to it:

1. You keep complaining about it, feel stressed and anxious, and start making excuses and blaming others.
2. You face it. You know that it already happened and you cannot go back in time to change it. You try to take it off your mind, make it toward your advantage and learn your lesson, and move forward and try to avoid making the same mistake in the future. You realize that the way you feel about it will not change what already had happened.

Try to always be a positive person with positive attitude, positive beliefs, and positive talk. Ultimately, you will spread positivity wherever you go and people will enjoy your presence more. However, by spreading negativity, you are only making things worse. Let's be real; only very few people actually care about the undesirable situation that you have been through. In fact, most people do not care at all. People may 'show' you that they feel bad because a bird has dumped on your car after you have just washed it, or you lost your phone at the food-court at a mall because you were thinking of how good will you look wearing that new dress you just bought. We all have our own problems to worry about. Keep in mind that I am not saying do not complain at all, or that there is absolutely no one that cares about you. We all feel the urge to let out our emotions sometimes, or want to share something with someone. But try to not complain about every little thing throughout your day that had annoyed you. Try to share what you feel only with the people that are really close to you, that will be understandable no matter how much you complain. People like to feel good. They like to be around people who make them feel good, build their confidence and self-esteem, and make them laugh. This is just our nature as human beings. We do not like people who spread negativity wherever they go and always complain about things. Let me give you a real-life example. Imagine that you see a person almost on a daily basis and that they are present in your environment and your surroundings for at least 1-2 hours daily. Whether it is a classmate that you attend similar lectures with them or a colleague at work that is in the department that you are. Every time you encounter this particular person, they just keep complaining about the traffic they had been at today when they were driving to work, or how slow their coffee machine was at brewing coffee this morning, or how long it took them to find something to dress before coming to work today. I refer to these type of people as **"the complainers"**. They just find something to complain about throughout their day. More importantly, they do not complain because they actually feel bad or stressed about something, they just complain because they simply feel the urge to do so. Slowly, you will start to avoid their interactions. You will try to avoid seeing them because you know that they will say hi and then just start their complaining championship. Try to not be one of these people and remember: 99.9% of people do not really care, **even though they may show you that they do;** avoid complaining.

Chapter 22

The Laws of Power

We have discussed in previous chapters of this book some of the laws of the universe, success principles, and some human psychology and behavior. In this chapter, I will share with you some of an essential personality traits and ways of approaching 'life' that will add up to your picture of developing a successful character. These traits were derived from Robert Greene, in his book, The 48 Laws of Power.

When I first read his book, I was surprised by his ideas and what he calls 'The Laws of Power'. What makes these laws unique is that they are not just laws on a surface level, meaning that in most cases, you will hear someone talking about making people obey someone or follow their instructions when they talk about power. However, these laws of power are different in that they examine power and authority on a deeper level that provides critical understanding of what makes people powerful. There are 48 laws of power in the book, but I will only mention 14 of these laws as I think these are the essence of the book and the most fundamental. However, that does not mean that the other 34 laws are not important; but the laws I have chosen are the ones that are most relatable and most commonly used in life real interactions.

Law #1: Never Outshine the Master

Always make those above you feel comfortably superior. In your desire to please or impress them, do not go too far in displaying your talents or you might accomplish the opposite – inspire fear and insecurity. Make your masters appear more brilliant than they are and you will attain the heights of power.

Law #3: Conceal your Intentions

Keep people off-balance and in the dark by never revealing the purpose behind your actions. If they have no clue what you are up to, they cannot prepare a defense. Guide them far enough down the wrong path, envelope them in enough smoke, and by the time they realize your intentions, it will be too late.

Law #4: Always Say Less than Necessary

When you are trying to impress people with words, the more you say, the more common you appear, and the less in control. Even if you are saying something banal, it will seem original if you make it vague, open-ended, and sphinxlike. Powerful people impress and intimidate by saying less. The more you say, the more likely you are to say something foolish.

Law #17: Keep Others in Suspended Terror: Cultivate an Air of Unpredictability

Humans are creatures of habit with an insatiable need to see familiarity in other people's actions. Your predictability gives them a sense of control. Turn the tables: Be deliberately unpredictable. Behavior that seems to have no consistency or purpose will keep them offbalance, and they will wear themselves out trying to explain your moves. Taken to an extreme, this strategy can intimidate and terrorize.

Law #21: Play a Sucker to Catch a Sucker – Seem Dumber than your Mark

No one likes feeling stupider than the next persons. The trick, is to make your victims feel smart – and not just smart, but smarter than you are. Once convinced of this, they will never suspect that you may have ulterior motives.

Law #28: Enter Action with Boldness

If you are unsure of a course of action, do not attempt it. Your doubts and hesitations will infect your execution. Timidity is dangerous: Better to enter with boldness. Any mistakes you commit through audacity are easily corrected with more audacity. Everyone admires the bold; no one honors the timid.

Law #30: Make your Accomplishments Seem Effortless

Your actions must seem natural and executed with ease. All the toil and practice that go into them, and also all the clever tricks, must be concealed. When you act, act effortlessly, as if you could do much more. Avoid the temptation of revealing how hard you work – it only raises questions. Teach no one your tricks or they will be used against you.

Law #32: Play to People's Fantasies

The truth is often avoided because it is ugly and unpleasant. Never appeal to truth and reality unless you are prepared for the anger that comes for disenchantment. Life is so harsh and distressing that people who can manufacture romance or conjure up fantasy are like oases in the desert: Everyone flocks to them. There is great power in tapping into the fantasies of the masses.

Law #34: Be Royal in your Own Fashion:
Act like a King to be treated like one

The way you carry yourself will often determine how you are treated; In the long run, appearing vulgar or common will make people disrespect you. For a king respects himself and inspires the same sentiment in others. By acting regally and confident of your powers, you make yourself seem destined to wear a crown.

Law #35: Master the Art of Timing

Never seem to be in a hurry – hurrying betrays a lack of control over yourself, and over time. Always seem patient, as if you know that everything will come to you eventually. Become a detective of the right moment; sniff out the spirit of the times, the trends that will carry you to power. Learn to stand back when the time is not yet ripe, and to strike fiercely when it has reached fruition.

Law #36: Disdain Things you cannot have:
Ignoring them is the best Revenge

By acknowledging a petty problem you give it existence and credibility. The more attention you pay an enemy, the stronger you make him; and a small mistake is often made worse and more visible when you try to fix it. It is sometimes best to leave things alone. If there is something you want but cannot have, show contempt for it. The less interest you reveal, the more superior you seem.

Law #38: Think as you like but Behave like others

If you make a show of going against the times, flaunting your unconventional ideas and unorthodox ways, people will think that you only want attention and that you look down upon them. They will find a way to punish you for making them feel inferior. It is far safer to blend in and nurture the common touch. Share your originality only with tolerant friends and those who are sure to appreciate your uniqueness.

Law #44: Disarm and Infuriate with the Mirror Effect

The mirror reflects reality, but it is also the perfect tool for deception: When you mirror your enemies, doing exactly as they do, they cannot figure out your strategy. The Mirror Effect mocks and humiliates them, making them overreact. By holding up a mirror to their psyches, you seduce them with the illusion that you share their values; by holding up a mirror to their actions, you teach them a lesson. Few can resist the power of Mirror Effect.

Law #46: Never appear too Perfect

Appearing better than others is always dangerous, but most dangerous of all is to appear to have no faults or weaknesses. Envy creates silent enemies. It is smart to occasionally display defects, and admit to harmless vices, in order to deflect envy and appear more human and approachable. Only gods and the dead can seem perfect with impunity.

Chapter 23

Focus on the Right Thing

When an individual wants to perform a task, there are often different factors that come into play that increase the likelihood of the task being performed, delayed, or never being accomplished. These factors are a combination of mental factors that subsequently influence physiological factors that lead to action. Examples of the mental factors include how motivated are you to achieve the task, how much value does achieving this task offers you, how exciting the end results are to you, how rewarding are these results, and how different your life will be than the current life you are living now once you achieve that task. You must put yourself in the right and suitable mental state in order to achieve extraordinary things.

The greater the task is, the more difficult it is for the mental factors to be in your favor. For example, take in person A and person B's tasks and goals:

- Person A's goals (the tasks that they would like to achieve):
  - ➤ They want to be physically active for a minimum of 80 minutes per week.
  - ➤ They want to work in a minimum-wage job from 9 to 5 every day.
  - ➤ They want to quit education after graduating from high-school.

- Person B's goals (the tasks that he would like to achieve):
  - ➤ They want to get into a worldwide body physique contest.
  - ➤ They want to earn a six-figure salary and aim to be a CEO in a well-known firm.
  - ➤ They want to pursue higher education and earn their Master's degree in their field.

Taking in these two scenarios (A and B), the amount of mental preparedness and psychological conditioning that is needed to accomplish person B's desires is much greater than is it for person A's desires. Person B has to be more focused, more motivated, and ready for harder work than person A. But as mentioned earlier; the concept of success is relative. You work harder and suffer more pain but ultimately you are rewarded more. If it was easy, everyone would do it.

Now the common problem here is that **most people focus on the wrong aspects while trying to accomplish great things.** This is a huge mistake that a lot of people fall into that eventually makes them start doubting themselves and start having these thoughts that may hold them back from proceeding further. Throughout the process of accomplishing our desires or goals, we start thinking about how tired are we; all the long hours of staying up late at night working on something. We start doubting ourselves and our capacity of getting the task done and start thinking: "It is harder than I thought". We just try to come up with suitable excuses that will prevent us from feeling bad about it when we quit. And you cannot blame yourself for this. Our brains are designed in a way to keep us comfortable; to spend the least amount of energy and effort. It is your will-power that gets you progressing. The reason that we mostly focus on the wrong aspect when we pursue a goal (being tired, complaining) is that because this is what are we experiencing at the moment. We cannot feel the rewards, yet. And this is the most significant and detrimental phase that differentiates average from extraordinary people.

Solution? All you have to do is focus on the outcomes and rewards that you will earn after you achieve this particular task rather than thinking about how much effort you had put in it so far, or how exhausted do you feel at the moment. Shifting your focus from negatives (current state) to positives (future outcomes and expected rewards) will fuel your desire, keep you motivated, and place you in a solid mental state that is unbreakable so that you can accomplish great things. Just change the direction of your focus and you will see how things become easier to achieve.

Chapter 24

The Big Trade-off

Every one of us have so many desires and goals that they wish to accomplish. The amount and 'size' of these desires vary depending on the individual. For some people, all they want is to live in peace and pay their bills, while others want to live to the maximum of their potential. They want to achieve all these great things in life that the average people do not even bother to think about. These great things may require time, hard-work, determination and consistency, but they also offer great rewards and value. You could say that as a general rule; the more difficult a task is, the more value it holds and vice versa. You could also say that the more value something holds to you, the more you are willing to do it. All of the great things in life are waiting to be accomplished; they just need you to prepare yourself and adjust yourself to the correct mindset and psychological state in order to reach it. No one said it is easy, but no one said it is difficult too; it is you who makes the decision. And this is what makes life great when it comes to being successful. Everyone is rewarded based on how hard they work, and everyone gets their fair share depending on their effort. This is also what differentiates people in terms of how hard they work. You can tell how much effort people are putting into their lives by examining their surroundings, their skills at life, their lifestyle, their mentality and way of thinking, and their way of communicating with people. However, there is an exception to every rule, and the exception to this rule is that we are only referring to the self-made millionaires and the people who became successful through their own efforts, not the people who inherited millions of dollars from their parents, or those who won the lottery.

I am not sure whether life is always fair or not, but what I know for sure is that life is fair when it comes to hard work and self-achievement. Your efforts are always proportionately rewarded in life. No matter how hard you work, you will always see a result. It may not be the result that you were expecting, but it will open the doors for other opportunities that you had never even thought of.

Throughout your life, you will always find yourself facing a trade-off between two decisions: to continue working on what you are supposed to be doing, or defer it for a later time because you do not feel like doing it now. **No matter which option you decide to go with, this trade-off will determine the quality of your whole life.** If you choose the first option, welcome to the club. But, if you decide to choose the latter option, you will mostly remain as you are for the rest of your life.

No one likes to stay up long hours past midnight to work on something; no one likes to be sitting for long hours daily for a long period of time trying to come up with a solution or develop a new idea; no one likes to work-out 6 days a week; no one likes to knock on people's doors in an attempt to sell a product to random people. So why do people do all these then? **Because they like living their desired life more than they hate the process of reaching it.** if you want greatness, you have to start sacrificing. Muhammed Ali, a world champion and one of best boxers of all time, once said: "I hated every minute of training, but I said, 'don't quit. Suffer now and live the rest of your life as a champion'.

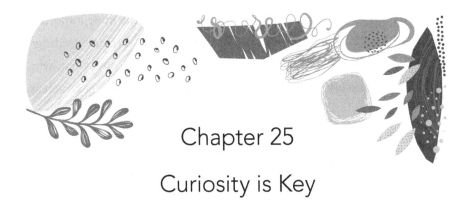

Chapter 25

Curiosity is Key

Throughout my life, I have always been a curious person. I wanted to be knowledgeable of my surroundings. Whether it was relating to my actions, other people's actions, events and life circumstances around me, wealth and financial status, or relationships and communication with others. I had something in me that had made me question everything around me. I kept on asking questions such as "what made this particular person act in that certain way"? or "what made this person react in that particular manner"? "why is that 80-year-old man standing beside the bus stop waiting for the bus when the temperature is -25 outside (considering I live in Canada, -25 is only 'a bit chilly')? Where is his car? Why isn't he using it? didn't he work hard enough during his youth? Or does he feel lonely and want to see and get engaged with other people on public transit?

Maybe this old man has a car but he just does not want to use it. maybe he is a millionaire but money still makes him feel lonely. Like it or not, we as humans like to judge people. That's just how the world works. Some people judge others for a few seconds then totally forget about it, while others take it to the extreme. It is not a matter of whether judging is good or bad, it is just how a normally functioning brain reacts to individuals that are similar to them. You may judge people internally; that is okay. But you must not behave with other people based on your judgement of them.

As I grew up, I realized that being curious was one of the most important features I had. You have to be aware of yourself and your surroundings. You have to be aware of how things work. You have to know what, why, and how things work. This will provide you with five advantages, such as:

1. By knowing what causes something, you are better able to reach your goals and desires. All you have to do is work on the causes.
2. By knowing what causes something to not happen, you will increase your chances of attaining what you wish to have or accomplish; as you will avoid doing it knowing that it does not work. Thomas Edison once said "I have not failed. I have just found 10,000 ways that won't work".
3. When you are curious and begin looking into human behavior, you are better able to predict people's actions and reactions. This will significantly improve your communication skills as you know what makes people accept or reject an idea or a proposal. You will also be able to view things from other people's perspectives, as you ask yourself for example, "what made them like/dislike a certain behavior or idea"?
4. You will clear, adjust and create the proper mindset to reach your goals. This will also increase your self-confidence and self-esteem as you know that doing A will result in B.
5. Knowing what causes something to happen will increase your control over your life. There is little space for randomness in your life.

Haven't you had enough of a life in which your circumstances are what decide your life rather than you deciding your circumstances? I mean, imagine it. How different your life could be if you knew exactly where you are going; if you knew how to do it; and what to do? How different would it be if you had full control over your life? Well guess what, it is possible. All you have to do is be curious, ask questions, and look for answers.

I have no special talent. I am only passionately curious- Albert Einstein

Chapter 26

Apply What You Learn

Have you ever wondered why so many people spend hours and hours on personal development yet they see little difference in their life? Everybody wants to be successful, and the majority of us are willing to do what it requires to be successful. You may read books, attend seminars, and listen to audiobooks of other motivational speakers or self-help experts, but you may get nothing in return. How is that possible? Allow me to answer the question on your behalf.

A large amount of people fall in the same mistake, which is simply **not applying what they learn.** For example, if you were watching a 20-minute YouTube video of Brian Tracy talking about time management skills and the importance of it. Then once the video ends, you turn off your device that you were using to watch the video and continue on your normal daily routine, without applying the concepts taught in the video. In that case, guess how much benefit have you attained from watching the self-help video? Zero. You are even equitable to a person who had never watched the video. Why? Because both of you and the person never watched the video had not undergone any effort to improve their time management abilities. The only difference is that you were more motivated and more willing to learn something new than the other person is.

We are often so busy and focused on knowing as much information as possible that we usually forget to apply what we have learned. You could have all the knowledge in the world and all the information you need to reach your goals. But if you do not use the information and put your knowledge into action, you will not reach your goals. It is like when you want to visit a friend at his house; you have your brand-new car parked in front of your house. You have the car keys and the car is in a fully functional state, but you just do not use it. Technically, if you want to go to your friend's house but you are not using your car; your car is useless. Just like the knowledge that you possess but not put into practice.

This is why self-development and improving yourself is a dynamic process that requires utilizing a combination of theory and practice in order to achieve maximum results. They are both equally important and work together for your benefit if used properly. Knowledge without practice will not get you much results, and the same concept applies to practice without knowledge. If you spend effort and work hard on something, but you do not know where are you going, or what are the ways of doing something, it is very difficult to achieve any progress.

Knowing is not enough. We must apply. Willing is not enough, we must do. – Johann Goethe.

Chapter 27

Positive Stress & Negative Stress

Stress is a common emotional state that occurs frequently throughout our normal daily life. In order to better understand stress and cope with it, you have to know what is it, what causes it, and why it emerges. The causes of stress may vary among individuals depending how much they care about something. However, it generally arises when we feel that we are facing an issue that is outside of our control that we do not have the adequate resources to deal with it. Whenever that happens, our brain releases neurochemicals to our physical and psychological body. As a result, this negatively impacts our mental capacities and functioning abilities that may reduce or impair performance at the present moment or in the future.

The degree at which stress may negatively affect our performance and mental functioning depends on what is causing the stress (the stressor), our perception of the stressor, and how we react to it. For example, stress levels would be highest when a student is writing a medical school final exam or for a pilot who is preparing to take-off or land an airplane. On the other hand, stress levels would be relatively lower when someone is driving on a highway or talk to a random stranger. The level of stress is not that important. What is very important, however, is the common false perception of stress as a 'bad thing'. Yes, stress may reduce your performance or impair your ability to think, or even make your heart beat faster when you think about the stressor and in all honesty, no one likes that. BUT, most of the negative impact caused by stress stems of our negative perception of stress, and if we change the way how we think about stress, we can change the way how we feel about it. Stress will occur either ways; whether we feel good or bad about it. It is a normal natural human reaction. **But you have to change your negative perception of stress in order to use it for your benefit.** And the first step in doing so lies within identifying the types of stress and what is the difference between them.

Stress can be categorized into two categories: negative stress (distress) and positive stress (eustress). Negative stress is the commonly known stress that most of us are aware of. However, it is only part of the equation.

Negative stress (distress) has the following attributes (Mills, Reiss, &Dombeck, n.d)

- ✓ Motivates, focuses energy.
- ✓ Is short term.
- ✓ Perceived as within our coping abilities.
- ✓ Feels exciting.
- ✓ Improves performance.

On the other hand, positive stress (eustress) has the following attributes:

- ✓ Causes anxiety or concern.
- ✓ Can be short- or long-term.
- ✓ Perceived as outside of out coping abilities.
- ✓ Feels unpleasant.
- ✓ Decreases performance.
- ✓ Can lead to mental and physical problems.

Through categorizing stress and identifying it, we will be better able to cope with stress as we know that not all stress is bad, and stress in some cases can actually enhance our performance, only if we knew how to use it for our benefit; and knowing that such positive stress exists is the first step to do so. Realizing that not all stress is bad, and that some stress is positive is able to significantly improve our perception of stress and therefore, improve how we cope with it.

Chapter 28

Write It Down

As we said in previous chapters, success is a multi-dimensional concept. There is no sole factor that leads to success. Rather, it is a combination of several attributes and mental states that combined, lead to success. However, of these success factors, there are factors that are more important than other factors, and that not all factors are equal. I am not sure to what prevents us from being successful, but I can assure you that **goal-setting** is one of the most essential factors of success.

When you set a goal, you are creating a direction for yourself to keep going forward. You are clarifying to your mind of what exactly is it that you desire. In that sense, your brain will generate an enormous amount of self-motivation for you to accomplish the task and reach your goal, because when you set a goal, you are providing the logical reasoning and the rationale to yourself. Your brain knows that the reason why you should work towards that particular thing is because you had specified it as a goal that you want to pursue. If you do not have a clear and a previously-set goal, you will feel lost. It will be very difficult to reach what you desire, no matter how hard you work for it. You may reach other destinations or end up in a decent position, but not the position that you had intended to be at. You may have the best knowledge and abilities and work the hardest, but still not become what you wanted to be. Why? Because you did not have something in mind to work for. You do not have a sense of direction. For example, if you have the most developed and technologically-advanced ship that is equipped with the latest technologies and engines, but the ship does not have a destination and it does not know where it is going, it will go anywhere, it will be lost in the sea. Having knowledge and mental capacities is not sufficient; you also need a target. Something that you would like to achieve or acquire.

After you have clearly-set goals, and you know exactly what do you want, you have to write it down. Write your goals on a piece of paper or on your phone's notes. It does not matter where you write it, what matters is that you write it. when you write something down and read it for several times, you are subconsciously imprinting it in your mind. Once imprinted, it will influence how you act towards it. It will start showing in your behavior, which will eventually, help you to turn what you have wrote into reality. Also, when you write down your goals, you translate your invisible thoughts into visible; something that you can see. You are transporting what you have in your mind into the physical world. All what you have to do now is apply it. Think about it this way, "if you know what you want, and have a plan of how to attain it, what else in the universe could prevent you from reaching it?".

Also, it is important to keep in mind that you have to pay close attention when you set goals for yourself. Goals should not be taken to the extreme. You have to balance your goal that it is not too easy that it barely requires you any effort (often has low to no value), nor it is too difficult that it will bring you de-motivation and frustration. However, research has shown that individuals who set setting specific, difficult goals are more likely to achieve their goals than those who set general, easy ones.

According to the Goal-setting theory, there are five key characteristics of successful goal-setting. Goals must be (Neutrino, 2012):

1. Specific: goals must be specific.
2. Measurable: goals must be achievable.
3. Achievable: goals must be achievable.
4. Realistic: goals must be realistic.
5. Timely: goals must be set within a specific time-frame.

Quote: if you fail to plan, you are planning to fail- Benjamin franklin

Chapter 29

Fear and Uncertainty

Have you ever had an honest moment with yourself and asked yourself, "what may be stopping me from being who I really want to be"? You know, we always have dreams and things in our minds that we want to translate into reality. Things that we want to have, experience, and add on to our lives. Things that we admire the most. But along with all of those, there comes a quick slight feeling of unreality. This little belief that whispers "common, you know you won't get there". But again, your solid determination and will-power re-takes control over things and you start getting closer to achieving your goals at even a faster pace. No one has ever said that they never doubted themselves throughout the process. Even the greatest champions and the most successful people have had their share of these temporary thoughts. There are always ups and downs along the journey, but it is only for those who have enough courage to keep on going.

Getting back to our previous question in the beginning, if you dig deep down and ask those people who want to start their own business, or go for a trip around the world, or even quit their jobs and look for another job, what is preventing you from doing so? Most of them will refer to **fear** as their answer. But if you think about it a little more; what is fear, really? We hear it and say it so often that we got to a point where we don't actually think about it anymore, we just express it. it is really the fear of the unknown. **We**

are afraid of what we don't know; because we, just don't know! We are afraid because we are not certain. Uncertainty is what produces fear that prevents us from being where we want to be. You are uncertain of whether your business will be successful or not. You are uncertain of whether you will find another job after you quit your current job; even if you do, you are uncertain if it is going to make your life better or not. You are afraid to make a decision because you are uncertain of whether you made the right decision or not, and the list goes on. However, if you think about it, uncertainty is actually a blessing. Not only uncertainty is a good thing, it is what adds value to this life and keeps it balanced. It is what keeps things going. How is that possible? Well, if we were certain and knew everything, we would be too bored of this life to a level that some people may not want to complete it to their 20s. imagine if you knew everything about yourself by the time you start developing consciousness. If you knew exactly how long are you going to live, how much money you will be worth, to what extent you will be successful and achieve things, etc. Will you really be interested in proceeding? A major life factor, uncertainty, is what gives flavor to our daily lives. Without it, we would even be de-motivated and unwilling to proceed to do any of these great things in life. And it circulates in every part of the universe. The student keeps wondering 'will I pass my exam'? 'will I be able to graduate and get a university degree'? subsequently, they work hard and do their best to answer their doubts with a yes. The employee wonders 'will I get promoted'? 'will I get a pay raise'? subsequently, they put extra effort and contribute to their company so that they answer their doubts with a yes; and so on.

We often have so much incorrect perceptions about things in life, but if we thought about it one more time, our perceptions will be different. Uncertainty must be an element of our lives, and fear is what keeps us going and fuels our determination and hard work. Trust me, you wouldn't want to be certain about your life; let's keep it that way.

Chapter 30

Widen Your Scope of Life

Every individual was born with different circumstances. These circumstances largely shape our lives. People who were born poor will likely not care as much about money as people who were born of a businessman/businesswoman parents. Or they may want to passionately make money because they were deprived from it during their childhood. Also, people who were born of parents who are doctors will most likely have an interest in medicine or become doctors, and the list goes on; I think you got the idea. The point is that we are born differently, and these variations are what keep this life balanced. You cannot have 7 billion people on earth in which the 7 billion of those really want to become millionaires. You also cannot have 7 billion people that are absolutely broke. Rather, we have the musicians, artists, athletes, businessmen, teachers, writers, philosophers, fashion models, etc. We have a little bit of everything, some of them compose the elite-class people in their field while others, with sufficient training, are on their way. Bottom line is that we have different interests. Do not use what are you interested in as a scale to measure people's abilities or potential. I remember when I was I kid, I used to instantly classify whoever I meet into two categories: the rich and the poor. As I grew up-and this is very important- I started to realize that not all people care about money. Not everyone wants to be wealthy. Some people would give up all the money in the world in a trade for a quiet rainy night with their painting brush and painting board. Others would value spending 2 hours playing on their violin passionately more than they value spending 2 days in a 7-star hotel. **Widen your view of life and do not narrow your scope of people**. Just because you are interested in learning how to make money that does not mean that everyone has to be interested in learning that too. We have to start accepting people as they are. Accept their values, beliefs, and interests. Not everything has to be money-related. Even in some cases, if you were good enough, you can make an enormous amount of money throughout doing what you like; you just have to be passionate doing it. I am a huge believer of money and wealth. But I am also a huge believer of that money shall not dominate your life and thinking. Try to earn money but keep in mind that life isn't all about money, and there are other important things. You have to make money work for you but shall never work for money. We live in a world today that you cannot live without money, at least to a level that you can cover your expenses of living. And let's be real, those who have the most amount of money hold the most authority and have the most power and control over their surroundings. This may not be a good thing, but it is just how things are going.

Accept what other people like and enjoy doing, and keep what you like for yourself. Even better if you find people who share similar interest than you do. This will put you in a constant development and improvement cycle where you can always share and exchange ideas and thoughts, as well as listen to what other people are saying and learn from them. Playing the role of the listener is very important, because it opens up the door for new ideas and opportunities that you have never thought of.

When you talk, you are only repeating what you already know. But if you listen, you may learn something new. – Dalai Lama, Buddhist monk

Chapter 31

The art of decision making

Throughout life, you will constantly come across situations where you have to decide on something. Regardless of how big the decision you will be taking is, the concept is always the same. Proper decision making is essential to succeed in life. It is one of the most fundamental skills that largely influences the quality of your life. The decisions that you make will alter your situations which in turn, alters your life. Throughout your life, you have to be aware of two things when it comes to making a decision: emotions and the outcomes of the decision.

➢ Emotions and decision making

When it comes to decision making, **you must set aside your emotions.** In some cases, we want to make an action solely based on our emotions- how the action will make us feel. In other cases, our emotions prevent us from taking an action. For both cases, the decision that you make that is based on emotions will most likely not be in your best interest. For example, you may really want to be driving a $50,000 Mercedes just because it makes you feel that you are rich, or it shows to other people that you are; where in fact, you aren't. if you decide finance that $50,000 Mercedes where you cannot really afford it and the expenses that comes along with it, but you did just because your emotions led you to do so, you made a wrong decision. And this decision will negatively impact your financial status on the long-term and force you to sacrifice buying other more important things just to afford the monthly payments of the leased car, if not put you on dept. do not get me wrong, I am not saying that do not buy nice cars, no. You can always buy nice cars but when you are in a financial-free situation where you are absolutely able to. This is just an example to make you get the idea, but it applies to almost all aspects of life when it comes to making a decision based on your emotions.

> The outcomes of the decision

Whenever you make a decision, **never think of the decision in the short-term**. Rather, think of the impacts of the decision on the long-term. Always double-think about your decisions before you make it. this will give you an extra advantage of ensuring that it is the right decision. But, how will you know that it is the right decision? Very simple. Next time you have to decide on something, have a pen and a paper handy and draw the following: write the decision you want to make on the top-middle side of the paper, and draw a vertical line separating the paper into two columns. On the right side, write down all of the pros that will result from making that decision. While on the left column, write down all of the cons that you can think of that will result from making that decision. Now after you have both the pros and the cons of the decision, weight the pros in relation to the cons. If there are more resulting advantages than there are disadvantages of making the decision, proceed with the decision. If the opposite is true, do not make that decision; as simple as that. Although this method may seem simple, it is one of the most effective and easiest ways to decide on something that will ensure you making the decision that is in your best interest.

Ultimately, you can always decide on what you like, ignoring considering your emotions and the outcomes. But you have to keep in mind that this will only bring you more trouble and make you struggle more throughout your life. You may not like a decision, but you will appreciate its true value once you see results of making the best decision. And remember, decision making is a habit, the more you make the right decisions the better you get at it and the easier it becomes later in life. A single incorrect decision may have a life-long impact that will negatively alter your life, and vice versa. Examples include marriage, studying abroad, changing who you spend most of your time with, career-related decisions, etc.

It is in your moments of decision that your destiny is shaped- Tony Robbins

Chapter 32

If you want to be successful, act like one

Being successful combines multiple characteristics and attitudes. It is not like something that happens overnight, or occurs as a result of a single factor. Rather, it is a set of factors that are imbedded in the individual. These factors are repeated frequently so that they eventually turn into habits. Therefore, **those who want to be successful in life have to act like it.** you have to embrace success in every aspect of life that collectively, make you up as successful personnel. Success has to be imprinted in your mind so much that it shows in your actions. As a successful person, you must always show up dressed neatly and elegantly. The way you dress shows so much about you as a person, and it is not like I'm valuing appearance more than intrinsic features, it is just that people base so much of what they think of other people based on their looks. No matter how open-minded someone is or has high consciousness, consideration of your physical appearance is still taken into account; it is just our brain's natural psychology. Keeping that in mind, the way how you speak is also another important factor. If you want to be successful, you have to speak like a successful person. Talk like you're already the most successful person you know. This has a huge positive impact and increases your chances of succeeding and reaching your goals as when you talk and behave like you are already successful, you are imprinting it in your subconscious mind. Done frequently enough, being successful will be so obvious and undoubtable to you so that eventually you will become one. "Fake it until you make it" kind of thing, it is very powerful; more than you can imagine. You have to factor in the concept of success into your communication habits. You also have to behave like a success. You can't just desire success but your actions say otherwise. You must wake up early, do your duties, and work hard towards your goal. You can't just sit on the coach watch TV and play video games all day then complain about not being able to succeed. It starts with as simple as always being on time, managing your time properly and allocating it in a way that is most beneficial to you. That does not mean you cannot have fun or have times for yourself, but you also have to work harder than you play. You must also expect to be successful in order to be one. You have to treat yourself like one. Avoid all the negative self-talk and the people that reduce your self-esteem. These won't get you anywhere. You do your thing and ignore everything else in the surrounding. This will keep you focused towards your goal.

All of these factors collectively fall into what I call it 'self-image'. Self-image is how you view yourself. It plays a major role in becoming what you want to become because the belief of being successful starts within you. If you do not believe that you are or will be successful, no one else will. **You must view your current self exactly how you want to be in the future.** This is very effective because if you do not act like a success from now, you will never be one. Act like you were born to be successful, like you are not just like everyone else. You belong to success, not to the average people. You must view yourself a superior from everybody in this planet. But pay very close attention to how you behave. Do not behave like you are superior of the people around you, keep this one for yourself. Do not let it affect your actions and always stay humble at all costs. And more importantly, love yourself and people around you will love you. Provide help whenever asked, and do not turn people down; you will need them someday.

Chapter 33

Stereotype is your worst enemy.

One of the biggest problems we face today is that people tend to stereotype. They just copy what others did seeking to get the same result. This may be a good technique in some cases, but mostly it must be avoided at all costs. The reason for that is that stereotyping kills creativity. It buries finding new and more effective ways to do something. It destroys innovation and makes it more difficult for someone to find their true self so that they can excel in their area of interest. It hardens the process of finding what you are good at, what do you like, what do you dislike, etc. I always say it to my friends and the people around me: "find your own way of doing something". Just because it is usually done in 'X' way by people, it does not mean that it is the only way. This is largely problematic in the educational settings. In university, someone may be really good at memorizing through writing the information on a piece of paper, over and over again. That particular person uses this strategy to study and it seems that it works perfectly fine with them, allowing them to attain good grades. Now on the other hand, their friend sees them using the strategy of repetitive writing in order to memorize information. They say to themselves, "well my friend is studies through the writing strategy and he earns good grades. It must be an effective strategy to memorize". After their next exam, they barely pass it, scoring a very low mark, then they start questioning their intelligence and cognitive abilities, without realizing that the problem does not lie within them, it lies within their method of studying. And all of this had occurred due to stereotyping. What works for someone may not work for the other. Be innovative, know what you are good at, and take advantage of your strengths and talents as a person. Another common situation where stereotyping is problematic is when parents in some certain cultures in the world decide on behalf of their children to be either a doctor, a lawyer, or an engineer. Parents should and must provide guidance for their children, as they are considered responsible for them until a point in their life. However, the idea of forcing children to specialize in a certain degree and not allow them to choose their own educational pathway is totally wrong. It destroys creativity and significantly limits the potential of advancement and development for many careers. When you deprive an individual from their freedom of choice of being involved in something, not only education, you will not get the best possible results. There will always be a margin of improvement, and things could be done in better ways. Why? Because you could be employing someone else in their field that had the perk of choosing that field, which in turn allows for better-quality results and more creative work because it was done with joy, passion, and free-will. The person chose to be there; therefore, they will produce. And when I say 'produce', I really mean it. This educational-career gap is destructive on so many levels. We must work collaboratively in order to close it; or at least, prevent it from widening. Imagine a world where everyone is doing exactly what they like and what they are good at. We would live in a world where we would have the best technologies, transportation, communication, construction, medical services, etc. that are best delivered.

Chapter 34

There is always a gray area

Many people view life as a binary area, where their perception of things is either 1 or 0; white or black. Meaning that whenever they think of something, it is either a yes or no issue; there is no place for somewhere in between. While in fact, life does not operate this way. It is an open-ended case where you can be doing both; having a little from each.

The problem is that the majority of people perceive life to an extreme. If they want to do something or engage in a certain behavior, they either want to be fully engaged or not engaged at all. This may work for some people, but it does not work for many others. It delays, if not prevents, people from be doing what they truly want to be doing. For example, if someone who is not physically active decides that they want to put their sedentary lifestyle to an end, and starts exercising. They set a plan to work out at the gym for two hours, five days a week. Unless they were equipped with a great amount of motivation and dedication, they will eventually fail to be keep on being physically active. They may continue to go to the gym for the first few weeks, or a month maybe, then they will stop. This is where the problem arises. The way our brains function is that they are created to keep us comfortable. Whenever our brain sees change, especially a major change within a short period of time, it will work towards preventing that change from occurring and returning to our original comfortable state, at all costs possible. This is why so many people are not able to bring huge changes to their lives within a short period. Rather, if we want to make changes in our lives and alter our current state, we must do it gradually. We must bring incremental change so that our brain and body are able to adjust to the new state and adapt to it, so that our brain and body could work with us to bring change, not against us. **Our perception of life as black-white is equivalent to trying to bring about huge change to our lives in a short period of time; it just makes things more difficult to achieve.** Returning back to our previous example of being physically active. If the person who had decided to be physically active starts exercising right-away, two hours a day, five days a week, it is unlikely that they will keep on engaging in the behavior (exercising), because their perception of being physically active is binary ("I either exercise or I don't"). in contrast, if the same person who had decided to be physically active decides to start walking for 10-minutes, on weekends only; they will have a very high chance of succeeding to be physically active and continue on what they are doing, because they are perceiving physical activity as a gray area ("I am not an active person, but that does not mean I cannot go for walks regularly or engage in physical activities; I can do both"). Once that person starts going for a 10-min walk on weekends, they may exercise at the gym for 30-mins, only on weekends. Eventually, it would be very easy for them to start exercising for two hours a day, five days a week, while in the first scenario, it is much more difficult.

When you view things as a 'gray' area rather than a binary approach, you are more motivated to keep on engaging in a behavior and it is easier for you to change a certain behavior because you are allowing time for yourself to adjust to the new behavior. Another example of viewing life as binary area is when someone who is used to wake up late at the day decides to wake up in the morning. If the person is used to wake up at 12:00pm in the afternoon and decides to start waking up at 7:00am in the morning every day, it would be very difficult for them to sustain their waking-up patterns

("I either wake up very late or very early", binary approach). While if the same person who usually wakes up at 12:00pm decides to start waking up earlier, and sets the alarm at 10:30am for the next week, then starts waking up at 8:30am for the following week; and eventually, starts waking up at 7:00am, it would be easier for them to make and sustain change in their life ("I could wake up few hours earlier, and then wake up a bit more earlier, until I'm used to waking up early", gray-area approach).

References

Greene, R., & Elffers, J. (2000). *The 48 laws of power*. New York: Viking.

Investopedia. (n.d.). 80-20 Rule. Retrieved from https://www.investopedia.com/terms/1/80-20-rule.asp

Kiyosaki, R. T. (2017). *Rich Dad, Poor Dad: with updates for today's world and 9 new study session sections*. Scottsdale, AZ: Plata Publishing.

Mills, H., Reiss, N., & Dombeck, M. (n.d.). Types of Stressors (Eustress vs. Distress). Retrieved from https://www.gulfbend.org/poc/view_doc.php?type=doc&id=15644&cn=117

Murphy, J. (2016). *The power of your subconscious mind*. Victoria, BC., Canada: Dead Authors Society.

Neutrino. (2012). What is Goal-Setting Theory? *GoStrength*. Retrieved from https://www.gostrengths.com/what-is-goal-setting-theory/.

Pease, A., & Pease, B. (2006). *The definitive book of body language*. New York: Bantam Books.

Robbins, A. (2013). *Awaken the giant within: how to take immediate control of your mental, emotional, physical & financial destiny!* New York: Simon & Schuster.

Standing, L. G., in *The SAGE Encyclopedia of Social Science Research Methods, Volume 1,* 2004

Printed in the United States
By Bookmasters